HOW TO STOP YOUR KIDS SENDING YOU BROKE!

HOW TO STOP YOUR KIDS SENDING YOU BROKE!

by

Sylvia Bowden

Published by Safehaven Ltd
35 Fantail Drive
Tauranga, New Zealand
info@silbo.co.nz
www.kidsandmoney.co.nz

ISBN 978-0-9876651-4-0

Editing, production & typesetting:
Andrew Killick
andrew@safelittleworld.co.nz

Illustrations:
Paul Smith at Blue Sky Creative
paul@blueskycreative.co.nz

CONTENTS

INTRODUCTION

'If you get your attitude towards money straight, it will help you straighten out almost every other area of your life.'
– Adapted from a quote from Billy Graham.

When my first book, *Parents – How to Stop Your Kids Going Broke*, was released, I received some intriguing feedback. A lot of people, upon reading the title, laughed and said, 'What I need is a book to stop my kids sending *me* broke!' So here it is!

Much of what's written here is common sense parenting, but we can all benefit from the wisdom of a wise old head! This book is based on personal experience and from observing other parents in action. I have also worked as a budget advisor and life coach, and have qualifications in counselling, adult teaching and training. My husband and I have had the privilege of raising two financially responsible young adults, and have come out of that experience financially unscathed! All this amounts to a wealth of practical information which I hope you can use in your own family situation.

This book is addressed to parents of children of all ages. No matter what age your child is, there's no time like the present to begin thinking about future-proofing yourself and your children.

With your financial future at stake, it is important to reflect on what the future holds for you and your kids. What sort of retirement are you hoping for?

From day one, your child looks to you to provide for them.

Unfortunately, for many parents, that pattern continues well after their kids leave school or start earning incomes of their own. If an adult child has expectations that their parents will constantly step in to make everything financially okay, the situation can become stressful and unhealthy for everyone involved. In order to put a stop to the constant hand-outs and expectations, train your kids from an early age to start thinking about money, how it works and how *they* need to look after it.

A parent is the greatest teacher in a child's life, either in a positive or a negative way. You can teach your kids a few principles that will help them stay on top of the money game. I say 'game' because, like all games in life, there are certain rules and principles that will make you more successful in what you do.

One such rule is: Prosperity, both financially and emotionally, is spelt with five little words – Spend Less Than You Earn!

Let's face it, we live in a society that encourages people to buy lots of stuff, and makes it extremely easy to get into dumb debt (borrowing for things that lose value) or to spend all your income without thinking about the future. As parents, we are sometimes as guilty of falling into this trap as anyone else.

But it is up to you whether you raise the kind of kids that send you broke or kids who are financially savvy and able to manage their own finances effectively.

You can pass on the 'rules of the game' to your children, helping them to become prosperous adults, and safeguarding the resources you have worked so hard for.

PART ONE:
Be a Super Parent!

Kids are like sponges – they absorb and learn a lot by what they see and hear every day. No one can influence your kids like you can. The things they learn by watching you in everyday life will help shape their habits as they grow into adults. So it starts with you! No pressure!

As parents, none of us are going to get it right all the time, but we should check the health of our own financial habits to set a great foundation for our families. To stop your kids sending you broke, let's begin with talking about you.

1. BE A GREAT ROLE MODEL

Your kids are watching you – you are their biggest hero! You are your child's greatest teacher, either in a positive or a negative way, especially when it comes to money. Let's get straight down to business with some practical aspects of being a great role model.

What sort of role model are you?

Ask yourself the following questions:

Do I read everything fully before I sign it?
Make sure you do – it's an important practice to model for your kids. If they fail to read the fine print in the future, that could have consequences for you if they end up in a jam as a result. (More about this later in the book.)

Do I have a spending plan (a budget)?
If your finances are in a mess, then your kids' finances could be too. Remember, they learn by example.

Do my kids see me sticking to my spending plan?
If yes, that's great; if not, then maybe it's time to start.

Do I pay my bills on time?
Spare a thought for the people you owe money to... How would you feel if people didn't pay you? If you are constantly paying your

bills late, your kids will think this is normal. The fact is, if they consider late payment 'normal', then one day they could be slow to pay you back if you have lent them money.

Do I lend my kids money because they overspend?
This is a major pitfall – avoid it like the plague.

Do I pay bills for my kids which they should pay?
Again, this can lead to a dangerous 'rescuing' precedent. Remember, your kids need to take care of their own responsibilities.

Do I pay their fines?
Definitely don't do this. It *will* send you broke, and risks 'rewarding' them for irresponsible behaviour.

Do I obey the rules set down by banks?
Banks put rules in place to protect you. An example of one such rule is, don't give anyone (including your children) your credit, debit or EFTPOS card and pin number.

> I know of a family who used to regularly give their EFTPOS card to their child to go into the dairy or supermarket for supplies. When this child grew up and had a boyfriend she gave him her EFTPOS card to go and get her something at the shops and he cleaned out her bank account, never to be seen again! This caused a lot of heartache and unnecessary stress.

Do I obey the law?

If you are a law-abiding citizen, you are setting a much better example for your kids!

Am I honest in my financial affairs?

Honesty is the best policy and will help keep your kids out of trouble. When tax time comes around, for example, do you declare all your income? Teach your kids to be honest when they deal with financial institutions such as the IRD and banks. With regard to tax, don't teach your kids that this is something to be avoided, but instead explain that taxes pay for important public services such as infrastructure, welfare, healthcare, education, and policing – things that make society what it is.

Do I give my kids money to spend without any training on how to use it?

Children need to learn from an early age how to look after money – training them in this area is one of your responsibilities. Don't leave it to the advertising and finance industries to educate your kids.

Do I use money as a tool to 'bribe' my kids?

If you continually offer money to your kids to get them to do jobs around your home (such as emptying the dishwasher) you will find this works quite well in the here and now. But think about the future, when they are older. This could backfire on you when you ask them to do something for you and they reply, 'It depends – how much are you going to pay me?'

Do I spend more money on my kids than time?

Sometimes parents who are very busy, hand out money in lieu of spending quality time with their children. This is sometimes motivated by a sense of guilt. They give their kids money and drop them off at the mall to spend it however they want. If this strikes a chord with you, then think about your work / family life balance. Time is the greatest investment you can give to your children.

Have I prepared them adequately for the inevitable – moving out of home?

Not just with money, but general life skills. For example, do they know the respective rights of landlords and tenants? I have witnessed some unjust treatment of young people because they did not know the laws relating to renting and have been exploited. Of course I have also seen the opposite – when young people don't seem to realise that their first priority is to pay the rent.

And all this adds up to the big question...

Are my kids KIPPERS (Kids in Parents Pockets Eroding Retirement Savings)?

I first heard the term 'KIPPERS' at a seminar I attended to do with understanding the 'y' generation and I think it's wonderfully descriptive. Are your kids dipping into your pocket and eroding your retirement savings? Are you raising kids that might be KIPPERS in the future? Now is your chance to change things!

> I am thankful that both my parents were excellent role models with regards to money while I was growing up.
>
> My dad taught me to properly read every document before signing it and to be honest at all times.

One day, when I was about 10 years old, I found a lot of coins under my dad's favourite recliner chair. They had fallen out of his pocket. I gathered them up and went to find Dad to return them to him. He said to me, 'Sylvia, because you've been honest by giving me back this money, I'm going to give you half of it as a reward.'

Another time, I was given too much change, so my mum sent me back into the shop to return the extra. The owner rewarded me by giving me a lolly. So what did I learn from these two experiences? Honesty pays off.

Sometimes you may not be aware that something you are doing innocently, or without much thought, could be contributing to your kids sending you broke. Sometimes you may even think you are doing the best for your kids, when in fact a different approach would be more beneficial.

I was told this story by a friend named Rose. She was at the supermarket with her husband and her two children, and gave her kids $10 each, as a treat, to spend on whatever they liked. After a bit of smart thinking by the kids, they worked out they could buy something better if they pooled their money – so now they had $20 in total to spend. The kids duly arrived at the checkout with a toy costing $29.99.

This was not an unusual situation, and Rose was about to add the extra amount to the shopping bill as she usually would. But, as she said to me, 'I remembered what you said about being a good role model, and suddenly wondered what my kids would learn from this situation.' She realised that by paying the extra $10, she could be teaching her kids to spend more than they had.

She told the kids they would have to put the item back, and go and find something for $20. Her husband was a bit embarrassed by the situation and initially wanted her to just pay the extra, but she stuck to her guns. So the whole family accepted the challenge, and together went around the store to find something that was $20 or under. They all ended up happy, and the kids learned a great life lesson: you can't spend more than you have!

2. EXAMINE YOUR OWN THINKING

If we are going to be great role models for our kids, we need to spend a bit of time on straightening ourselves out! We need to look at the way we think about things (including money) and how our thinking influences what we do.

The first step to uncovering what you believe about money is to think about your thinking! When you hear yourself talking about money, consciously take stock of what you are saying. Is what you are saying irrational? By 'irrational' I mean not clearly thought out and based on reality.

The truth is that the beliefs you hold deep down about money will influence how money enters and leaves your life. Your beliefs about money and everything else have been formed in four ways. 1) From the things you hear. 2) From the things you see. 3) From your life experiences. 4) From your parents, culture, society, media, teachers and the advertising and lending industries.

> We have become so well adjusted to our culture of spending that we do it without a second thought.

A common false belief regarding money is that 'money is the root of all evil'. If you believe that deep down, think for a moment how that could influence the way you handle your finances.

Perhaps you will spend money as fast as you get it – because you don't want to handle that evil stuff! This myth has developed over time from a misquotation of a verse found in the Bible, which says, 'The *love* of money is the root of all evil.' Money can't be inherently evil – it's a neutral thing that can be used for good or bad. Some people will do evil things to get money, but money can also be about freedom, choice, generosity, empowerment, value and goodness.

Money can be anything you decide it is – a tool to achieve great things, power in your pocket, a dirty piece of paper, a ticket to freedom, a ticket to unhappiness.

The question here is, what do you believe about money deep down in your subconscious? It is your deeply held beliefs that will affect your day to day relationship with money and influence how you spend money on yourself and your kids.

This is a huge subject which can't be adequately covered here. I recommend T. Harv Eker's book, *Secrets of the Millionaire Mind*, which can help you understand more fully what a big part our thinking plays in how we handle money. Eker believes that we all have a personal 'money blueprint' ingrained in our subconscious minds, and it is your blueprint that will determine your financial life.

The words we speak and the thoughts we have are powerful things! I used to wonder why some people seemed to go round and round in circles with regard to getting out of debt. One thing I have noticed is that people who constantly say, 'I'll never get out of debt,' invariably never get out of debt.

Have a think about the following statements and see if you recognise any beliefs that you hold, which may cause you to overspend. These are just a few statements to get you thinking about your thinking – you might be aware of some other thoughts and motivations that are hindering your finances more than they are helping.

- I must give my kids the things they want because I missed out as a kid, so I don't want them to miss out too.
- I can make my kids happy by giving them things.
- What will people think of me as a parent if my kids don't have the latest gadgets or clothes, or if my kids can't attend a big event?
- I want my kids to like me. They will like me if I give them things.

There's nothing wrong with wanting to get your kids involved in lots of activities and buying them stuff. However, if you don't have the income to do this, trying to live up to everyone's expectations will send you broke. It won't be the kids' fault – you are the adult – you are the one with the power to say yes or no.

Remember, many people of influence have grown up without the best of everything, such as Nelson Mandela, Abraham Lincoln and Oprah Winfrey.

To be happy, you don't have to have the best of everything, you have to choose to make the best of everything you do have.

Money personalities

Over the years, there has been a lot of research into 'personality types' that affect your outlook on life. Studies have also shown that people mainly exhibit one of several money personalities. The money personality varies from person to person. Knowing how your money personality functions in your life may give you an understanding of why and how you – and others – handle money.

To explain six of the different money personalities I will use animals as a comparison to help get the point across. It can be a fun exercise to guess what money personalities other family members might be.

The Aristocrat – Cathy the Cat. Cathy thinks money isn't important and can't be bothered worrying about it. She has far too many other important things to do.

The Saver – Silbo the Squirrel. Silbo loves to save for things he wants to buy, and in case he needs money for something unexpected.

The Hoarder – Harry the Hamster. Harry hates to spend money and finds it very hard to share what he has. He often goes without something important just to avoid spending his money.

The Spender – Mike the Monkey. Mike is so busy having a good time that he often spends more than he earns and is usually broke before next pay day.

The Avoider – Dizzy the Duck. Dizzy Duck dives for cover the minute the bills arrive. She is always late in making payments and ends up having run-ins with debt collectors.

The Safety Player – Timid Thomas the Mouse. Thomas is so afraid of making a mistake that he avoids making any financial decisions – even small ones.

So which money personality do you most closely identify with? You could be a mixture of more than one. Be careful about saying,

'I was born like that so there isn't anything I can do about it.' It helps to be able to identify your financial tendencies using the categories above, but you have a choice to be financially well or financially sick.

The way you think about finances and money will have a big impact on your decision-making processes. So let's look at some ways to make good decisions.

As the saying goes, 'There are two sides to every story.'

In my experience as a counsellor and budget advisor, I have found that saying to be true.

When making decisions about your finances (including making purchases) it is best to look at things from at least three points of view. Draw three columns on a piece of paper and write down these headings: my view (view 1), the salesperson's view (or my kids' view!) (view 2), an outsider's view (view 3). Then put yourself in each of those person's shoes and write down how they would look at it.

View 1 – The way you look at it. This view will be influenced by many different things such as past experiences, upbringing and what is important to you.

View 2 – The view of the person wanting to sell you the item (or it could be your child wanting you to buy them something – kids can be excellent salespeople!). This view will be influenced by things such as the commission he or she may earn or what advertising your kids have seen.

View 3 – When considering an outsider's view, ask yourself – is this person a sensible money manager and consider if they would gain anything personally from the decision you are about to make. Are they going to give you an unbiased opinion?

Often a third person's view can help you step back and take some emotion out of the equation. When making major financial decisions, be prepared to get expert and unbiased input from someone you trust. It can save costly mistakes!

3. CHECK YOUR THINKING ON DEBT AND SAVINGS

Nothing can impact our financial situation like debt and savings, and yet, we can get pretty blasé about both. We live in a consumer society where purchasing and spending is promoted as a way to be happy. The 'easiest' way to get what we want, when we want it, without having to wait, is through consumer debt. But what are we letting ourselves in for, and what are we doing to our families by taking on debt?

The lending industry

The lending industry, and in particular the credit card industry, has confused our thinking about credit.

Words on staements	What the lending industry want you to believe	Rational thinking
Credit card limit	How much money I can spend	How much debt I can get into
Your available credit	How much I have left to spend	How much more debt I can get into
Your annual interest rate	It won't cost me anything to use my credit card if I pay it off in full	If I can't pay it before the due date, it is going to cost me a heap more

As the table on the previous page shows, there is a difference between how lending organisations want us to think about credit and how we really should be thinking about it.

I like buying things when the price has been reduced. So when I was out shopping for some winter clothes and saw a sign that said, '30 percent off,' I was drawn to it! I saw a top that I really liked marked at $29.99. With the 30 percent off, it would only cost me about $21.

I went to pay cash for the top but was told it would cost me the normal price of $29.99 unless I made the purchase using the store's credit card. So in reality, the special was only available for people who were prepared to use credit.

I asked the sales assistant, 'How much interest will you charge if I don't pay the bill by the due date?'

'I don't know, but all I know is the interest rate is higher than a Visa card. You can find the information out on our website,' she replied.

Why would a store do this? Why would they only give you a discount if you put it on their store credit card? Wouldn't it make more sense to take the cash? After all, 'cash is king'!

Stores that offer these cards have done their homework. I have been told that some stores that offer cards make more from their finance department than they make from their cash sales over a year. Why? Because many people over-spend and are unable to pay off the balance owing when the bill arrives. These people can end up paying a whopping 20 percent more for what they purchased. That's why stores encourage you to buy now, pay later. No wonder our thinking has become confused; a credit card account has the potential to get us into a lot of debt!

It's almost compulsory to have a Visa or MasterCard these days, especially if you are making purchases online, but teach your kids to avoid credit cards and to use debit cards instead. A debit card provides much more protection from over-spending.

At the point of sale, a debit card functions the same way as a credit card but it takes the funds directly from your bank account instead of from a credit account. When your bank account is empty and you try to put a purchase on your debit card it will simply say, 'declined'. You have used up your available money. In the heat of the moment, when your emotions are high and you really want something, a debit card could help protect you from making poor financial decisions, and prevent you from getting into debt that will affect you in the future.

I can't afford to buy it unless I pay it off over time

This is such a dumb statement if you really think about it. Let me be blunt. If you can't save the amount per week to buy an item using cash, then how are you going to pay off the same amount each week with a loan, which will cost you more because of interest and administration costs?

False prosperity is having lots of 'things' that you still owe money on. Many people fail to realise that when you borrow money you become a slave to your lender.

Consumer debt can be like climbing into a swamp full of leeches that are sucking the financial life-blood out of you and your family.

These leeches also seem to have the ability to crawl from one generation to another. They need to find fresh blood – so they crawl and latch on to your children, and grandchildren, unless you take action and kill those blood suckers once and for all.

Recently I read an item that appeared in the *Bay of Plenty Times* with the heading 'Retail credit spending catches boomers out'. The article explained that the 'baby-boomer generation' had been persuaded to put items such as flat-screen TVs and holidays on their mortgages. As a result of the use of this kind of credit, the credit check agency Veda Advantage was noticing a massive increase in defaults for those in the 44 to 62 year old age group. The figure had soared by a massive 19.37 percent in the previous nine months.

The article stated that redundancy may have been a factor in this increase, although that was hard to prove. The managing director of Veda Advantage had warned, a year before, that 'interest free – two years to pay' deals would create problems, and it appeared that his predictions were now coming true.

I regularly meet people from this age group who use the 'I can't afford it unless I pay it off' excuse. I mentioned the problem with this kind of thinking earlier, but let's look at this statement in more detail, and examine how irrational it is.

To pay cash for something you need to save for it. That's pretty obvious really, but it's worth spelling it out. For example, if you want to buy a flat screen TV for around $2,000, you will need to save the following amounts per week: $38.46 a week for one year, or $19.23 a week for 2 years, or $12.82 a week for three years. So, ask yourself – can I save those amounts? If you are unable to save those amounts every week for one, two or three years, then how can you pay a hire purchase of the same amount, even if it is interest free?

The truth is that you have decided that you want that flat screen TV (or whatever it is) right now. You don't want to wait and save for it. That's the real reason why we put items on credit.

$38.46 may not seem like a lot to find every week for some people. However I know from experience as a budget advisor that if your financial situation changes, then $38.46 can mean the difference between eating meat or not eating meat each week, or being able to afford to pay for an activity which your kids love.

Everything sounds more enticing and affordable when you break it down to a weekly or daily amount. $38 per week or $5 a day sounds a lot more attractive than $2000 a year! But you need to always remind yourself of the total amount. Salespeople and hire purchase companies will often try to distract you from the total cost. And kids have been known to use similar tactics!

Imagine you're standing in the appliance store, admiring a flat screen TV, and your child says, 'But Mum and Dad, it's only $5 per day and we'll save money because we won't have to go to the movies.' Tricky little customers!

When your kids use these tactics, I don't think they learn anything if you just answer, 'We can't afford it.' Use this as an opportunity for a real live maths lesson. Get them to calculate the total cost and get them to imagine what it would be like if they had to spend that much money out of *their* savings or pocket money!

Buy now, pay later and interest-free deals

Don't get sucked into interest free deals to buy things for your kids or yourselves. Here are some points to bear in mind:

- Banks and finance companies use your money to make their money.
- They are a business and want to take your money!
- Make the system work *for* you and not *against* you...

> Interest free deals are interest free but they aren't cost free.

Before you rush out and get that amazing deal on 'no deposit' and 'four years to pay', stop and think about what the deal is really costing you.

Below is the real cost of an interest-free deal I looked into when our TV broke down. As I said before: Interest free? Yes. Cost free? NO!

That's 11.35% more than if you paid cash! So, stay away from 'buy now, pay later' finance deals – and even more so if it is your kids who are encouraging you to buy the latest gadget for them.

Sales people are trained to overcome your objections as to why you don't want to spend your money. If you have a weakness for impulse buying, then I suggest you say to the salesperson, 'I'm not purchasing right now as I have a '24 hour rule'. If I still want to buy it in 24 hours, after consulting my savings and spending plan, I'll come back.'

I have found from experience that when I tell a retailer about my savings and spending plan (more about that later), they are often a bit stuck for words! I don't think it's a response that they hear very often.

Go broke 'saving' money

A few weeks ago I saw an eye-catching sign hanging in a women's clothing shop which said **'SPEND TO SAVE 25%!'**

Talk about a contradiction in terms! One of the dictionary descriptions of the word *save* is 'to accumulate money'. One of the dictionary descriptions of the word *spend* is 'to pay money'.

The words *spend* and *save* are opposites. Spend = **pay**. Save = **accumulate**. However, retailers use these words together to get people to spend because they want customers to think they are actually saving. It makes a person feel less guilty about spending if they feel like they are saving at the same time.

Our thinking (our 'belief system') is lying to us if we honestly think we can save money while spending money.

When you buy something on sale at a reduced price – you are not actually *saving* money, you are *spending less* than the original advertised price.

Advertisers will appeal to your emotions to get you to buy. It is a good idea to let your emotions subside, and then decide, before spending your money. Remember, it is the advertising industry's job to make you want to buy something, and tapping into your emotions is one of the most powerful tools they have. It is your responsibility to make good choices with the money you have.

Clever marketing has changed our perception of reality. We say things like, 'I bought a pair of shoes for half price! I saved $50!' Your belief (that you saved $50) most likely came from a mindset communicated to us, over the years, by advertising. We can change our thinking by making honest statements. So instead of saying, 'I saved $50,' instead say, 'I spent $50 less than the original price by buying my shoes on special.'

A number of years ago I went on a tour holiday to Singapore, Bangkok, Hong Kong and Manila.

When I arrived in Singapore, I was overwhelmed by how cheap things were, especially electrical goods, so I went a bit crazy, buying up large because I was 'saving' so much money.

At the end of the day, I was comparing purchases with others on our tour. One of the guys said something to me that I will never forget: 'Singapore is the only place in the world that you can go broke "saving" money.' His comment really made me reassess what I was doing. I thought, he's right. If I spend more than I have, then I'm going to end up broke. I won't really be saving because how can I be saving if I end up without any money?

Debt trap

We all know that debt is a bad thing, but we aren't necessarily aware of just how terrible it can be. It can take a major physical and emotional toll, and causes so many family problems. Christians Against Poverty (www.capnz.org) is an organisation that specialises in helping people get out of debt. A survey that they conducted revealed that 79 percent of their clients skipped meals because of debt, and 36 percent of their clients had thought about or attempted suicide because of the stress they were under. So, do all you can to keep dumb debt out of your family.

Dumb debt (consumer debt) is borrowing for things that go down in value. Smart debt is borrowing money for things that will make you money. But all debt has to be handled with wisdom and caution.

Here's a story of a young couple I met while I was a budget advisor. They were following the 'New Zealand dream' of owning their own home. Taking on a mortgage can be an example of 'smart debt' but their story shows that the decision to go into debt should always be taken with extreme caution.

When I met this young couple, they were thinking that they had no option but to go bankrupt. They had gone to a bank about three years previously to enquire about the best way to save for their own home. The bank 'sold' them a large loan based on the fact that the husband's annual salary often included up to an extra $20,000 per annum overtime and the wife had a part-time job. The bank had looked at a few pay slips and advised them that they could buy now. The bank also consolidated some of their existing debts in the mortgage package.

The couple was excited to purchase their own home because, at the time, they had no problems meeting their outgoings. However, input from another person such as a budget advisor might have helped them look at the dangers and pitfalls of what they were about to commit to. A third person may have asked questions such as, how will you make these repayments if your overtime is cut, or how will you manage if you have children, or why have you got debt that needs to be added into your mortgage?

When the economic climate became more difficult, the husband's hours were cut back due to lack of work. Not all stories have a perfect ending. At the time I spoke to them, this couple's only option was to sell their home for considerably less than the amount owing, leaving them financially 'up the creek without a paddle'.

Real Saving

I often hear people say, 'I'll save when I have enough money.' What they really believe deep down is, 'I won't ever have enough money to save, so I'm not even going to try.' If you hold this belief, saving will be very difficult for you.

Any amount of money you can put aside, no matter how small, is enough to save. The habit of saving money is more important than the actual amount. So what do I mean by 'saving' in this context? Ultimately, this is about putting money aside for your retirement.

Having money available for expected and unexpected expenses, as part of sticking to a spending plan, is a different type of saving. Saving towards retirement is long term saving, and putting money away for expected and unexpected expenses is short term saving.

> My sister, who was a solo parent at the time, made a decision to put every 50 cent piece she received into a piggy bank for her son (my nephew). Together they made a papier-mâché money pig. The amount grew and was a great boost to her son's bank account. It was also a wonderful example for him to follow.

Habits are incredibly powerful things. When my nephew got his first job, the habit my sister had installed in him continued. He saved for a deposit on a house instead of buying the latest technology. He set his mind to fully paying off his home as soon as he could. He achieved this when he was 32 years old. He is now married with two children, and his wife is able to stay at home by choice because they don't have the burden of a mortgage hanging over their heads.

My sister believed that saving was essential, so this influenced how she handled her money. Her belief came from our parents and from the culture at the time, which instructed people to save up and pay cash for the things they wanted and needed. That belief was passed on to her son.

> Make saving for your own financial future a priority.

If you learn to spend and save according to a well thought-out spending and savings plan, you give your kids (and yourself!) an important advantage after they leave home.

PART TWO: Run a Tight Ship

The way you run your household finances will have a big impact on whether your kids can or will send you broke. It's all about putting systems in place that help to ensure your current and future financial stability. Kids that grow up in a financially responsible household will be much more likely to go on to be financially responsible adults. Get them involved in the day to day business of living, and avoid the common pitfalls of money at the same time.

1. HAVE A HOUSEHOLD SPENDING PLAN

> If you don't want your kids to send you broke, teach them to stick to your spending plan instead of *you* trying to live up to *theirs!*

What is a household spending plan (aka budget)?

What comes to mind when you think about budgeting? If having a budget immediately conjures up thoughts of going without and missing out on fun, you are starting on the wrong track. There is no downside to having a budget.

Basically a budget is simply a recorded calculation of what money comes in and what money goes out. It tells you how much you are spending and how much you are earning. At the end of the day you will either have some money left over or you will not have enough. Getting your spending to be less than what you are earning is called balancing the budget. To get your budget to balance it may mean that you have to do one of two things. Either increase your income (eg try and get some overtime or even consider additional work or even drastically find a better paying job) or alternatively, look at ways to decrease your spending or outgoings. Cutting down on little treats such as the number of takeaways or coffees might be all it needs to get your spending plan to balance. Another thing to look at is the cost of your utilities such as phone or power as there may be a cheaper company

> *A household budget is simply a plan for telling your money where to go instead of wondering where it went!*

than your current supplier. Another more radical way is to completely do away with the expense of the second car. As blunt as it may sound - It is essential to reduce your outgoings so they end up being less than your income. If you discover you have unmanageable debt, then please get outside help. Many communities have free services to help.

Most people love to spend, so think of a budget as a 'plan to spend'. Think of saving as a 'plan to accumulate money to spend in the future'.

The key to creating and maintaining a spending plan that really works is planning ahead. I have noticed that the most common mistake people make is they think budgeting is the same thing as getting a bill and trying to work out how to pay it from their next bit of income. This is not budgeting! This is called 'living hand to mouth' and it creates a lot of stress.

A 'household' is defined as a group of individuals living in a common dwelling. A 'household spending plan' covers each individual (including family pets) as well as expenses for the actual dwelling.

Having a household budget is simply having a plan for telling your money where to go instead of wondering where it went!

An effective spending plan needs to consider regular expenses (such as rent or mortgage) and to save for expenses in the future (such as tyres for the car).

Never before has it been so important for people to learn to budget. The important thing is not how much money you earn, it is what you do with what you earn that determines your financial future. If you don't want your kids to send you broke, you need to have a spending plan that you stick to, while teaching your kids to do the same.

Last year I wrote the New Zealand Household Budget Kit (published by New Holland), which gives full instructions on how to make an effective household spending plan, and how to stick to it. It is available to purchase from our website www.silbo.co.nz, or direct from the publisher at www.newhollandpublishers.co.nz .

The upside of having a household spending plan

Apart from helping you to teach your children how to manage finances for the household, a spending plan also allows you to:

- Avoid money pressures (which research has shown contributes to 89% of all relationship breakdowns)
- Be in control of money, instead of it controlling you
- Reduce stress
- Plan day to day spending
- Plan to save
- Plan to share (donate)
- Plan to invest
- Plan for the future
- Make informed decisions based on facts

> 'Wisdom makes the decision today that it will be comfortable with tomorrow. Emotion does what feels good today and takes no thought of tomorrow.' – Joyce Meyer

Many people have become so well-adjusted to the culture of spending more than they earn, that they do it without thinking.

How can I encourage participation in creating a spending plan for our household?

If you say to your kids, 'We want to have a family meeting to discuss living within a budget,' they will run a mile! But if you say you are having a meeting so that everyone can have some input on how to spend the money that comes into your house, you will find they will be much more receptive!

Once the final household budget is set, and the children have been involved in the process, you can address requests for extras much more easily. When a family member (including yourself!) asks, 'Can I have this?' the next question should be, 'Have we planned for it in our spending plan?' Having a plan, and sticking to it, will teach your kids great money management skills for now and for the future.

What does a household spending plan look like?

The first stage in setting up a household spending plan is to assess the financial situation of each individual member of the household. Let's look at a sample 'Fact-Finding Form' (on the opposite page) adapted from the *New Zealand Household Budget Kit*. This form is for 'John' – a young adult, employed but still living at home. It doesn't include the costs for the dwelling such as phone, rent or mortgage, power, insurance, repairs etc. The dwelling has its own separate fact-finding form, as do the other members of the household (including the family pet). The results of these individual forms are then applied to a 'Master Household Budget' (on page 49).

Facting-Finding Form

Name: John Date: August 2013

NET INCOME

Record the amount that lands in your bank account after all deductions (tax, superannuation contributions, student loan repayments, child support, etc.) have been take out.

INCOME (AFTER DEDUCTIONS)	$ AMOUNT	HOW OFTEN	DATE DUE	$ WEEKLY	BANK A/C
Wages/salary	548.46	W	Tuesday	548.46	2
Self-employed income*					2
NZ Super					2
Student Allowance					2
Government support (benefits)					2
Bank interest					2
Investment income					2
Child support rec eived					2
Family help					2
Other income					2
TOTAL WEEKLY NET INCOME				$548.46	2

Transfer this total to the Master Household Budget form beside your name under **INCOME FROM INDIVIDUALS (NAME)**. NB If you are a boarder or young adult living at home, your income is not recorded on the Master Household Budget form, just what you bring to the household budget in the form of board or contribution.

* Self-employment wage paid from business or holding account.

OUTGOINGS

ACCOMMODATION*	$ AMOUNT	HOW OFTEN	DATE DUE	$ WEEKLY	BANK A/C
Board	120.00	W	Wed	120.00	2
Share of rent/mortgage					2
TOTAL				$120.00	

* Complete this section only if you are flatting, boarding or a young adult living at home.

SAVINGS	$ AMOUNT	HOW OFTEN	DATE DUE	$ WEEKLY	BANK A/C
Special wants (eg, new camera)					3
House deposit		Y	Variable	50.00	4
Vehicle					4
Retirement					4
Holiday	1000.00	Y	June	19.23	3
Education					3
Family weddings					3
Just in Case money (JIC)	520.00	Y	Variable	10.00	3
Other					
TOTAL				$ 79.23	

PERSONAL FOOD	$ AMOUNT	HOW OFTEN	DATE DUE	$ WEEKLY	BANK A/C
Takeaways	15.00	W	Friday	15.00	1
Lunches	50.00	W	Mon – Fri	50.00	1
Dinners out					3
Snacks					1
Other					
TOTAL				$65.00	

UTILITIES	$ AMOUNT	HOW OFTEN	DATE DUE	$ WEEKLY	BANK A/C
Mobile phone	10.00	M	1st	2.31	3
Mobile broadband					3
Other					
TOTAL				$ 2.31	

EDUCATION	$ AMOUNT	HOW OFTEN	DATE DUE	$ WEEKLY	BANK A/C
Continuing education					3
Tertiary fees					3
Books					3
Other					
TOTAL				$	

TRANSPORT	$ AMOUNT	HOW OFTEN	DATE DUE	$ WEEKLY	BANK A/C
Vehicle licensing	147.80	6M	1/6 & 1/12	5.68	3
Warrant of Fitness	40.00	6M	1/6 & 1/12	1.54	3
Buses/trains/taxis					1
Petrol/diesel	75.00	W	Fri	75.00	1
Diesel mileage					3
Vehicle maintenance	600.00	Y	Variable	11.54	3
Vehicle insurance	160.50	Q	1/3 1/6 1/9 /12	12.35	2
Other					
TOTAL				$ 106.11	

DEBT REPAYMENTS	$ AMOUNT	HOW OFTEN	DATE DUE	$ WEEKLY	BANK A/C
Vehicle payments					2
Hire purchase (1) stereo	45.19	M	6th	10.43	2
Hire purchase (2)					2
Personal loan					2
Credit card (1)					3
Credit card (2)					3
Store card					3
Unpaid bills in arrears					2
Other					
TOTAL				$ 10.43	

SHARING WITH OTHERS	$ AMOUNT	HOW OFTEN	DATE DUE	$ WEEKLY	BANK A/C
Regular charitable giving (1)	10.00	W	Tuesday	10.00	2
Regular charitable giving (2)					2
Regular church giving					2
Other donations					3
Birthday presents (for adults)	52.00	Y	Variable	1.00	3
Christmas presents (for adults)	52.00	Y	Dec	1.00	3
Other					
TOTAL				$ 12.00	

HEALTH	$ AMOUNT	HOW OFTEN	DATE DUE	$ WEEKLY	BANK A/C
Doctor	104.00	Y	Variable	2.00	3
Chemist					3
Optometrist					3
Dentist					3
Ongoing medical expenses					3
Other					
TOTAL				$ 2.00	

INSURANCE	$ AMOUNT	HOW OFTEN	DATE DUE	$ WEEKLY	BANK A/C
Health					2
Life					2
Contents*					2
Other					
TOTAL				$	
* Enter contents insurance amount if you have a policy separate from the dwelling, eg, you are flatting.					

PERSONAL GROOMING	$ AMOUNT	HOW OFTEN	DATE DUE	$ WEEKLY	BANK A/C
Toiletries					3
Shampoo					3
Skincare/make-up					3
Hairdresser/barber	208.00	Y	Variable	4.00	3
Other					
TOTAL				$ 4.00	

CLOTHES	$ AMOUNT	HOW OFTEN	DATE DUE	$ WEEKLY	BANK A/C
Workwear					3
Footwear 2 @ $45	45.00	6M	Jan/Oct	1.73	3
Socks 6 @ $10	60.00	Y	Feb	1.15	3
Underwear 6 @ $12	36.00	6M	Jan/Oct	1.38	3
Sleepwear					3
Swimwear 1 @ $25	25.00	Y	Jan	0.48	3
Tops/shirts 6 @ $30	90.00	6M	Jan/Jul	3.46	3
Pants/jeans/shorts 2 @ $45	45.00	6M	Feb/Aug	1.73	3
Skirts/dresses					3
Hoodies/jerseys 2 @ $85	85.00	6M	Jan/Jun	3.27	3
Jackets/coats					3
Headwear/gloves					3
Formal wear					3
Accessories					3
Sports clothes 1 @ $113	113.00	Y	Sep	2.17	3
Other					
TOTAL				$ 15.37	

DISCRETIONARY SPENDING	$ AMOUNT	HOW OFTEN	DATE DUE	$ WEEKLY	BANK A/C
Cinema/DVDs					3
Other entertainment					3
Sports equipment					3
Hobbies					3
Spending money for self	30.00	W	Fri	30.00	1
Gym fees					2
Subscriptions					2
Other					
TOTAL				$ 30.00	

OTHER EXPENSES	$ AMOUNT	HOW OFTEN	DATE DUE	$ WEEKLY	BANK A/C
Bank fees	5.00	M	Last day th	1.15	2
Storage					3
Parties/celebrations					3
Other					
TOTAL				$ 1.15	

SUMMARY (OUTGOINGS)

Take the total **$ WEEKLY** amount from each of the tables above and write the amounts beside the categories in the table below. Then add up the columns to find your **TOTAL WEEKLY OUTGOINGS.** Transfer this total to the Master Household Budget form under **PLANNED SPENDING FOR INDIVIDUALS (NAME).**
NB If you are flatting or boarding, your personal budget is separate and your outgoings are not entered on the household budget.

COMBINED TOTALS	$ WEEKLY
Sharing with others	12.00
Savings	79.23
Accommodation	120.00
Personal food	65.00
Utilities	2.31
Debts	10.43
Transport	106.11
Education	
Health	2.00
Insurance	
Discretionary spending	30.00
Clothes	15.37
Personal grooming	4.00
Other expenses	1.15
TOTAL WEEKLY OUTGOINGS	$447.60

BANK ACCOUNT ALLOCATION

BANK A/C	$ WEEKLY
No. 1	170.00
No. 2	153.93
No. 3	73.67
No. 4	50.00
TOTAL	$447.60

This total should be the same as Total Weekly Outgoings.

Surplus / Deficit

Subtract **TOTAL WEEKLY OUTGOINGS** from **TOTAL WEEKLY NET INCOME.**

TOTAL WEEKLY NET INCOME	548.46
TOTAL WEEKLY OUTGOINGS	447.60
Surplus / ~~Deficit~~	$100.86

NB This figure does not take into account household expenses for the dwelling as the dwelling has its own fact-finding form.

Master Household Budget

INCOME FROM INDIVIDUALS (NAME)	$ WEEKLY
Dave (Dad)	589
Sue (Mum)	423
TOTAL	$ 1012

PLANNED SPENDING FOR INDIVIDUALS (NAME)	$ WEEKLY
Dave (Dad)	160
Sue (Mum)	175
Russell (brother)	53
Moggy (pet)	17
TOTAL	$ 405

COMBINED INCOME TOTALS	$ WEEKLY
Dwelling (John's board)	120
Individuals	1012
TOTAL HOUSEHOLD INCOME	$ 1132

COMBINED OUTGOINGS TOTALS	$ WEEKLY
Dwelling	556
Individuals	405
TOTAL HOUSEHOLD OUTGOINGS	$ 961

FINAL CALCULATION	$ WEEKLY
Total Household Income	1132
Total Household Outgoings	961
TOTAL INCOME MINUS TOTAL OUTGOINGS	$ 171
If income is more than outgoings you have a surplus. If outgoings are more than income you have a deficit.	

On the sample form, under the 'how often' heading, you will see a set of abbreviations have been used: D = daily, W = weekly, FN = fortnightly, M = monthly, Q = quarterly, 6M = six-monthly, A = annually, and E = estimated.

Also, you will see columns named 'bank account', which are numbered 1, 2, 3 or 4. This system is based on having separate accounts for different purposes. It is a way of dividing up your income so that each part is set aside for a particular use. My husband and I use this system to manage our own household finances and it really works. A similar system, using jars instead of bank accounts, can be used with your children's pocket money to teach them good financial habits – more about that later in the book.

Following the sample fact-finding form, I have provided an explanation of each account that we use at home, along with some hints about how you can use them effectively. In our household, we've replaced the number four account with a superannuation scheme for long-term savings, but we'll look at the other three more closely.

No. 1 account – cash

This account is used for the things that are paid for on a day to day basis – such as groceries, lunch money, petrol and leisure spending. It can be very helpful to withdraw the amount of money you have budgeted in this area and use paper money throughout the week. I'm not from the the dinosaur age – eftpos (debit card) and internet banking are great! But it is easier to track how much you are spending when you're using notes and coins than if you are using a card. You might be tempted to access your overdraft when using an eftpos card (or perhaps not even be aware that you are about to go into overdraft), but with cash, when it's gone it's gone!

It takes a real mind shift to use cash again but it prevents you from overspending. Be realistic about how much you will need for day to day expenses. Sometimes, if you run out of cash during the week, you'll just have to make do.

Some people have told me they don't want to use cash because they feel unsafe carrying it around. However, if you plan ahead and spend most of your cash on the day you withdraw it (for things such as groceries, petrol and giving your kids their lunch money) you won't have a big wad sitting in your purse or wallet.

Hints for operating your No. 1 (cash) account: Use the eftpos card on this account once per week. Do your grocery shopping and at the same time take out the rest of the cash you have pre-allocated. If you find that you have more in your shopping trolley than you can afford without going over your budget, swallow your pride and put something back on the shelf. If you have more money to pay the bill than you need, keep that extra amount for next week. Ultimately, surpluses and shortfalls should balance out – if they don't, you need to go back and revisit the original estimates that you used to set up your spending plan.

No. 2 account – automatic payments

I describe this account as the DNT (do not touch) account. This is where our wages are deposited each week. I set up all my automatic payments from this account for expenses such as mortgage payments, home and car insurance premiums, and rates. I even set up an automatic payment to a charity I donate to once a year. These automatic payments ensure that the money is going where it needs to go and that bills are paid on time. Paying your bills on time will save you money, as many utility providers allow for a prompt-payment discount.

On one occasion, before I used automatic payments for our utility bills, I paid our power account one day late, because we were away on holiday. It cost us an extra $59.61! That was all the incentive I needed! I now pay a set amount each week by automatic payment (the power company advised us how much to pay by working out an average based on previous usage). This fixed weekly amount makes it easy to stick to a spending plan. During the summer months our power bill shows a credit but this is used up as our consumption increases during the winter. Because we make a fixed weekly payment, we never miss out on our prompt payment discount.

Insurance and other payments are often cheapest if you can pay them annually in one lump sum and in advance. If you are able to make those large one-off payments, then that is the best way to go. But, realistically, many families won't have enough money in the bank to pay an annual amount. In this situation, I think the extra you spend by paying bills on a monthly basis far outweighs the stress of trying to find an annual lump sum.

Many companies will want you to pay by direct debit. When you authorise a direct debit, you are putting the utility, finance or insurance company in charge of how much you pay – they are able to change the amount of the payment and take it out of your account without your intervention. But I prefer to pay a set amount by automatic payment because that puts me in charge of how much I pay. This allows me to budget more accurately and be fully aware and in control of the amounts that are leaving my account. I recommend you do the same.

So if a company pushes for a direct debit arrangement, stick to your guns and insist on paying by automatic payment because it will make it easier for you to keep to a spending plan.

Aside from automatic payments for regular bill amounts, I also set up automatic payments to transfer funds from the number two account to our other accounts. So, our wages go into our number two account, then fixed weekly amounts are automatically transferred to our number one (cash) account and our number three (planned and unplanned expenses) account. You will possibly also have a number four (long-term savings account for specific goals, such as a house or car), so you can set up an automatic payment to transfer this amount too. The diagram below shows how this works.

After you have made these transfers, the amount left in your number two account must be enough to cover anything you

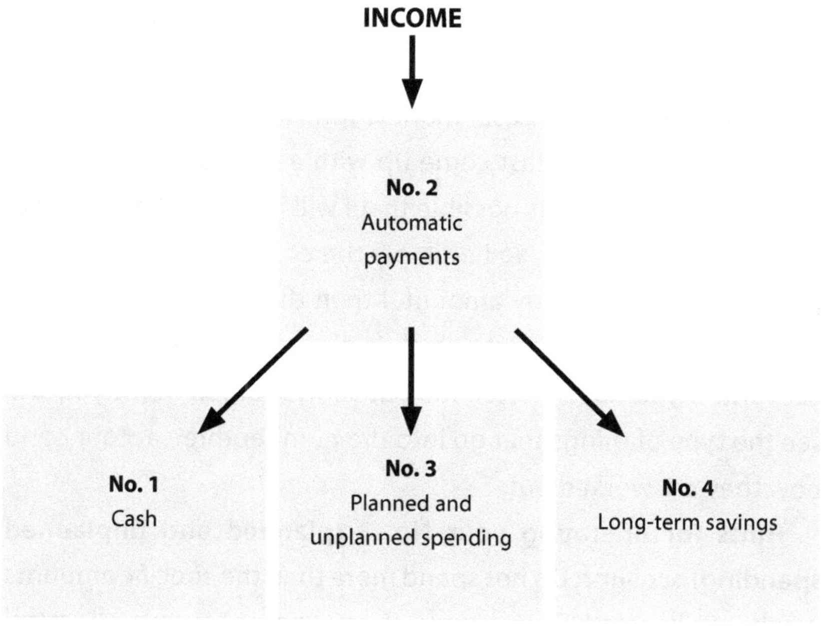

have set up to be paid automatically. If you get paid fortnightly or monthly, you can still use the same system. Use the Fact-Finding Forms to break everything up into weekly amounts.

Hints for operating your No. 2 (DNT) account: Sometimes this account has a very healthy balance, so it can be tempting to draw money out for extras and promise you will pay it back before your next automatic payment is due. But remember, all the money in there has an assigned use. The healthy balance in this account is often misleading because it will reduce dramatically when a series of monthly payments come out around the same time. That's why this is called the 'do not touch' account! If you keep that rule in place, and make sure your automatic payments are set up accurately, you will never miss the due date on a bill again.

No. 3 account – planned and unplanned spending

This account is for planned and unplanned spending, such as doctor and dentist fees, money for clothes, personal grooming, car repairs and JIC (just in case) money. You can plan for most items of expenditure or at least come up with a pretty close estimate. For example, I think it is possible that I will need to go to the doctor four times per year, so I multiply the cost of one doctor's visit by four to get the yearly amount. I then divide that figure by 52 to find the weekly amount, which is placed in the number three account. If you have a close look at John's sample form you will see the type of things that go into the number three account and how they are worked out.

Hints for operating your No. 3 (planned and unplanned spending) account: Do not spend more than the specific amounts you have allocated. For example, if you know you have allocated the funds to get your hair cut six times a year at $30 per cut ($180 per year at $3.46 per week), don't go to a salon that charges $50. Or if you've put aside $35 per month for takeaways, don't spend $40. These extra expenses might seem minor at the time, but ultimately they will sabotage your spending plan.

Again, be realistic when planning. For example, plan for repairs, tyres and ongoing car maintenance. I used to allow as much as $600 per year for car repairs for our second hand car. If a year goes by and you haven't spent your annual amount for repairs or maintenance, you will inevitably be hit by a big repair bill sometime in the future – so let the amount accumulate from year to year. Also, be realistic when planning for JIC (just in case) amounts – always be prepared.

General hints: I have two eftpos cards (one for the number one account and one for the number three account) and I have labelled them 'Account No. 1 (cash)' and 'Account No. 3 (planned and unplanned expenses)'. I have also made our number three account a visa debit account so that I can make online purchases. I don't need a card for the number two account (automatic payments) because this is the DNT (do not touch) account.

How does this all work practically?

Is it really that easy to run a tight ship? I have found that using this system makes it very simple to manage household finances. The system takes a little effort to set up, but it is effort well spent and it will ultimately save you time, money and stress.

How does this work when self employed?

If you run your own business, it is important to separate personal and business expenditure.

I suggest you set up a 'holding account' for your business and pay any income you receive into this account. Then pay yourself a set wage each week from that account into your personal No. 2 account (automatic payments). You will need to work out how much your business can afford to pay you (we used our accountant to help us here). Be realistic. Make sure you leave enough money in your business account for business expenses and tax. Check with a professional advisor to make sure that this is best for you and your business.

Before we utilised this system, we made the mistake of taking random personal drawings out of our business account. Everything turned to custard when our annual tax bill was due and we didn't have enough money left in our business account to pay it.... lesson learnt!

2. APPLY SOME COMMON SENSE

At the launch of my first book, *How To Stop Your Kids Going Broke*, my local Member of Parliament, during his speech, said, 'Sylvia, your book is a lot of common sense. Unfortunately common sense isn't very common any more.'

Sometimes common sense is all you need to stop your kids sending you broke. So here are some everyday tips that will help you stay financially well.

Don't let your kids eat you out of house and home

Kids need fuelling up. The amount of food your family consumes can make your shopping bill huge. So, what can be done?

When you go to the supermarket, take a fixed amount of cash with you and stick to a planned dollar amount for groceries. Shop once per week, and stick to that schedule. Don't make repeat visits to the supermarket throughout the week.

Make use of the freezer to prevent food going off. Keep an eye on wastage. Remember, when you throw food out, you are throwing away money.

In our household, we divide items such as bread rolls, loaves of bread, bacon, etc, into smaller amounts and freeze those into meal-sized portions.

We freeze even small amounts of leftovers rather than leaving them in the fridge where they inevitably get thrown out. I call these frozen foods our 'free meals'. They are very handy when we are busy or have had a tiring day, and reduce the temptation to buy takeaways. Sometimes we each sit down to a different 'free meal'.

I know it can be difficult to only shop once a week when you have growing children, but I also know from personal experience that it can be done. Planning a menu ahead of time and sticking to the fixed amount for groceries are the keys to making this work. Do your shopping list *before* you go shopping, not as you wander around the supermarket. Eat before you go shopping – it's a well-known fact that when people are feeling hungry, they buy extras.

Once the shopping is brought home, you will probably need to set some ground rules. We used to tell our kids, 'It's your choice; if you choose to eat all the treats (like biscuits, juice etc) in the first couple of days, that's up to you, but when they're gone, they're gone.' Pretty soon, the kids found that if they made the treats last, then they would still have some left towards the end of the week.

It won't harm your children, or you, to only eat a certain amount of food each week. So don't rush out and top up the fridge throughout the week. You will be doing your kids a favour health-wise, as well as safeguarding your long term financial future. This new situation might be hard for your children at first, but they will soon get used to it.

Obesity has become a major health issue in many countries and I believe one of the contributing reasons is that many people just keep filling their fridges when the kids or another member of the family says, 'There isn't anything to eat.' Often the truth is that there *is* food to eat – just not the goodies that they want to eat.

Talk with your children about why you are shopping differently. Get them onside, and dare I say it, even get them to help with the shopping list and weekly menu.

Keep a tally of your purchases on a calculator as you walk

around the supermarket to ensure that you're on target to shop within the amount you have allowed.

Don't be too proud to put things back on the shelf if you go over your allocated spending amount for groceries.

Let your emotions subside before deciding to spend your money

We touched on this subject earlier in the book, but let's investigate it a little more as it is very important.

It can take as little as 10 minutes in a store to sign up to buy something on credit which can then take months or years to pay off.

Since the recession has hit, retailers are offering sale items more than ever. If you have saved up for something and are checking out prices before you purchase, then this can be a great time to buy. Your hard earned money will go further than it used to. However, these offers are just as likely to tempt you to make an unplanned purchase.

As I mentioned earlier, advertisers will appeal to your emotions to get you to buy – they are very good at it. Have a look at some of the following phrases I have picked out from adverts:

Low price...
Free $40 grocery voucher with xyz purchase...
Introductory offer...
25% extra free...
Purchase a xyz and receive a 43" LCD TV valued at up to $1000...
November only...
Win a xyz Christmas hamper. Helping everyone save for a magical Christmas...

Protect your investment now...
Win 1 of 3 trips to Paris plus you'll receive a free underlay...
Interest free - pay nothing for 48 months...
Looking for a special night out...
Win a $1000 shopping spree...
The ultimate Christmas gift...

It can be an interesting family activity to watch all the adverts on TV and discuss each one, trying to identify what tactics the advertisers are using. This trains your children to read between the lines and recognise adverts for what they are. Let's face it, if the advertiser can get your kids to pester you to spend your money, then their job is done.

A fun way to carry out this activity is to write the following words on separate pieces of paper: repetition, use of fear, popularity, being new, humour, jingles, music, health and well-being, feeling good about yourself, 'you deserve it', lack of something, power, freedom, sex appeal, something free, comfort, security, value, fun, convenience and excitement.

Give each person one or two of these words or phrases and get them to identify adverts that use those tactics to encourage you to buy. You can also record the adverts and discuss each one, looking for the hidden meanings that the advertisers are communicating.

Kids can be taught to question what advertisers and retailers say. Ask questions such as, 'Where is the real evidence that to be popular I must have this particular brand or item?' The human psyche is very powerful and advertisers have studied the best ways to influence it so that we spend our money on stuff. But because our psyche is so powerful, we can also turn it around on the advertisers and critique their claims and methods.

You might be starting to wonder if I'm on some sort of mission against retailers! I promise I'm not; in fact we used to own a small grocery shop ourselves, so I understand that everyone is trying to make a living. But I want to point out the tricks of the trade so that you can be an informed customer who can spot the truth of the claims that are made in advertising and marketing.

Stand up to 'But other kids...' or 'Other parents...'

Kids will sometimes pressure you to buy things by comparing what you do to what other kids' parents do. You need to watch out for this and be strong!

The beginning of the school year can be an expensive time if you let your children dictate what they should have because 'everyone else has it'. When my children were younger I can still remember the pressure I felt when they would say, 'But Mum, the teacher says...' or 'But Mum, my friend has a really cool school bag' or 'So and so's parents let her, so you're really mean if you don't let me.'

> Of my two kids, it was my son who would get especially irritated by my refusal to conform to the crowd. On one occasion, he insisted that he had to have his exercise books covered in Duraseal. The product was so expensive that it cost more than the exercise books themselves.
>
> We sat down together and worked out the costs for different alternatives such as brown paper, cutting out a picture from a magazine and putting it on the front, and Duraseal. My son called me a cheapskate, hoping I would change my mind. In the end, a compromise was made

by thinking outside the square. I suggested that we just put Duraseal on the fronts of his books, which halved the cost. He was happy as his books had Duraseal covers and I was happy because I managed to stay within the budget I had allocated for new school stationery!

Washing, washing, washing

One thing that will help stop your kids sending you broke is to cut down on the amount of clothes washing you do.

I am amazed at how much washing some families generate. What I have noticed is that parents are often quite successful at getting their children to put dirty clothes into a basket or washing hamper. But many children put items in the washing basket that have been worn for a short time after school and aren't dirty at all. Some families unnecessarily wash pyjamas and towels every day.

We once caught our kids putting freshly washed clothes into the washing basket because they couldn't be bothered putting them away. I know my kids aren't the only ones who have tried that trick!

A bit of forethought and education about when clothes actually need to be put in the wash can stop your kids sending you broke and save you a considerable amount of money and time.

You might be wondering why I've identified the laundry as such a drain (excuse the pun!) on household finances. Think about the cost of the washing powder, electricity to run the machine and the cost of the water, if you pay for water usage. Some families use a clothes drier in winter, which increases the power bill significantly. Then there is the wear and tear on the machine and the clothes to consider. Your time is also a valuable resource. Think about how long it takes to do the washing, hang it out (or put it in the drier), iron it (if you're into that), then fold it and put it away.

I did some research and found that it costs me 62 cents per wash to do a load of washing. That includes the cost of the water, electricity and detergent. It would be more if I used fabric conditioner or washed in hot water. That amount doesn't include the cost of repairing or replacing the machine. (Remember, the more you use your machine the quicker it is going to break down.)

Your kids can send you broke and use up a lot of your time if you are continually doing washing when the clothes really aren't dirty. Sixty-two cents per load might not sound like a lot of money but even if you only do one load per day, that adds up to over $226 per year.

Showers

Hot water is expensive. The longer the shower, the more it costs. Your kids can send you broke if they refuse to get out of the shower after a reasonable length of time.

> Our son was a serial offender when it came to having long showers. In fact, most times he would drain all the hot water. I'm not one to give up easily and sometimes I get a little worked up about these things. I tried knocking on the door, pleading, setting timers, etc – all to no avail. My husband is much quieter than me, he just said to our son, 'If you aren't out of the shower when your

time's up, I'm going to turn the water off at the front gate.' Sure enough, the next shower came and our son was well on the way to exceeding his time limit. My husband went to the mains tap and turned it off. Our son emerged from the shower, not at all happy and still a bit soapy. We had to do that twice more over the following days, but our son finally got the message, which reduced our power bill considerably.

A bit of patience saved us $114

I've included the following story because it is a good example of how you can think outside the box, do your 'homework' and find a cost-effective solution when you need to spend money – common sense in action.

I ran over my laptop power cord with my desk chair. As I untangled it from the wheel, I noticed I had damaged it beyond repair – the cord had been stripped to the wire and, of course, it was the end that had the transformer attached.

My husband and I (as he is much better than me at dealing with technical stuff) headed to two different well-known electrical stores to find out if we could buy a replacement cord. We were quoted $146 for the replacement cord.

Now, I can be a bit impatient sometimes. I wanted to buy the replacement right there and then, especially seeing as the staff had been so helpful, and I didn't want to be without my computer. But my husband is more patient and he wanted to do some more research.

So we left the store and I was feeling a bit frustrated. But my husband was looking forward to checking prices on the net and perhaps finding a secondhand cord on TradeMe.

After about 20 minutes searching online, he found a wholesale supplier that supplied exactly what we needed for $27 plus $5 freight. Once the supplier had the money, the part was shipped overnight. We spent $114 less by doing some research and having some patience.

Let's analyse this. How many hours would I have had to work to save $114? Supposing I earn $20 per hour after tax, then I would have to work nearly six hours to gain $114. So in effect, the $114 less that I had to spend had an equivalent value of six hours of work!

Here's a formula to bear in mind if you want to spend less money: Facts x Time x Patience = SPENDING LESS DOLLARS.

Remember, it is not how much money you earn which will determine if your kids will send you broke – it is what *you* do with what you earn which will determine your financial future.

3. GET CREATIVE

When we're faced with a financial difficulty, we need to be creative about finding a solution. Creativity is a wonderful thing to pass on to your children – it helps them become problem-solvers and innovators. Often, when we find a creative solution so that there isn't such a high financial cost, we discover something truer than things that money can buy.

One of the best opportunities for a family to share quality time and create great memories is during the holidays. It is wonderful when people make a real effort to get together at times like Christmas. But these traditions, or the expectations that go with them, can become expensive. Renting accommodation, eating out, and buying the latest gadgets or toys can be a stressful drain on financial resources. The excitement of the holiday you had will be short-lived when the bills arrive, or you find you have run out of money for necessities, such as paying the registration on your car.

If you plan for a holiday like this and it is catered for in your spending plan then that's great. If you don't have the money in the bank to spend on holiday costs though, stay home.

If you are a family who has been affected by unemployment, or a reduction in income, I urge you not to be tempted to give in to those old beliefs such as 'we have always done it this way, so we must do it this way' and being worried about what other people will think.

If you're not able to afford a holiday, find alternative ways to enjoy yourselves – it's time to get creative. As a family (which can be a couple without children), sit down and do some brainstorming about how you could do the Christmas or holiday season differently this year. Write down everyone's ideas – whether those ideas will work or not. Look in the newspaper or on local websites to see what there is to do for free. Ask other people how they entertain themselves in the holidays. Out of this brainstorming and research process, you will probably find things to do that will create brand new memories and experiences for the family. Here are a few ideas to get you thinking:

If you have a tent, could you all live in your backyard for a holiday at home, or put your tent in the back yard of a friend or extended family?

House swapping is another cost-effective solution. As they say, a change is as good as a holiday!

One year, when our family was young and we got together with other relatives, we decided to make a 'mini golf course' in our back yard. We planned out the route around the house, put obstacles in the way, made the hole flags, and carefully dug a small hole in the lawn for the hole so the grass could be put back later. We had two putters which we got from somewhere. We had competitions between the boys, the girls, couples etc. It was loads of fun and kept us entertained for days.

When my son was five years old, my family decided to have a family reunion in Western Australia. I was very fortunate as my five brothers and my sister pooled their money and paid for me to go from New Zealand.

As it was around school holiday time, I wanted to take my son with me so he could meet my family and so I could spend some time doing special things with him. He was what could be termed 'a strong willed child' and I felt the need to try and build a better relationship with him as we often had disagreements!

I really spoiled him on this holiday. I spent a lot of money taking him to places such as the zoo, Water World, a science museum for kids, and wildlife parks.

At one of the markets we bought a boomerang. He asked if we could go to the local park and play with it. I didn't really want to, but he nagged me and I finally gave in as I thought about the reason why I had bought him on my holiday.

We spent a couple of hours throwing and catching this boomerang. To my surprise, I quite enjoyed myself – particularly when I saw how much *he* was enjoying it.

When we returned back to New Zealand, many people asked him what his favourite thing was about his holiday in Australia. He told everyone, 'Playing with a boomerang with my mum in the park.'

I learnt an important lesson from that experience. More than anything else, my son wanted my time – he wanted me to interact with him. Apart from the cost of the boomerang, it was the cheapest thing we did while on holiday. It was a great holiday and we did lots of fun things, but that trip to the park was the best. I could have saved a huge amount of money by spending time with my child doing something that he wanted to do right here in New Zealand!

When I realised how important it was to him that I spent time with him, I started to make an effort to play with him more. He is now 26 years old, and the good relationship that was forged through those times still continues.

There is a saying, 'The most important thing you can spend on your children is time.' It is so true. And the best thing about spending time with your kids? It doesn't send you broke!

4. PROVIDE THEIR NEEDS BUT NOT ALL THEIR WANTS

This is a short chapter, but it's important. Talking about our purchases as *wants* and *needs* helps us to determine how crucial it is that we have a particular item, and helps us spend more carefully.

As we've seen, it's always good to give ourselves a reality check. As humans, what are the basic things we need for survival? Anthropologists have defined these things as: Food, clothing, shelter and love. The basic truth is that they are the only things we *need* in order to live. Looking at life this way puts everything else – all the other luxuries and things we *want* – into perspective.

In the western world, we've done a wonderful job of convincing ourselves that a vast number of things that we want are things we *need*.

Once I asked a group of people, 'Is a fridge a want or a need?' Without hesitation, they all answered that it was a need. But imagine you were living in Japan at the time of the earthquakes and the tsunami. You escape with your life. Now ask yourself, is a fridge a want or a need? Ultimately, it really is a want.

When my parents were first married they didn't expect to have a fridge. They saved up and bought one to make life easier after they had already saved for and bought their first home.

In our modern society, wants and needs have become confused. Once again, this is in no small way due to the efforts of the advertising and lending industries. But regardless of how effective their message is, it is up to you to let your emotions subside before deciding to spend your money.

If you are continually saying, 'I need this' or 'I need that', then your subconscious is placing too high an importance on things that may actually be optional extras. The result is that you may buy things you really just *want* because you think you *need* them. Talk about wants and needs with your family. Discuss items around your home and categorise them as a need or a want. Become aware of how you speak about things you would like to have.

There is nothing wrong with having wants if they are planned for. Just be honest and call them what they are – wants.

PART THREE: Be Smarter than Your Kids!

A lot of the things we do as good parents will have a positive impact on all areas of a child's life – including financial health. So let's look at some parenting practices that will train them up for the future, and help ensure that they don't deplete your resources when they grow up.

1. LEARN TO SAY NO!

Do you ever find yourself saying 'no', then five minutes later changing it to a 'yes'? Think before you change your decisions – your kids will respect you more if what you say is well considered and final.

In the heat of the moment, when your kids are asking you for something that costs money, sometimes you need to answer, 'Let me think about it.' This gives you time to consult your spending and savings plan. My go-to response with my kids was often, 'I'll have to check with Dad first.' My husband would respond to the kids in the same way, telling them that he would have to check with me. Kids quickly learn to go to the parent who is the softest touch, but our kids learned not to try and play us off against each other because our policy was always the same.

Sometimes it helps to confront your kids with a decision based on what they are asking for. For example, 'If we spend money on going to the movies, we won't be able to buy takeaways this week. Would you prefer to spend our leisure money on the movies or takeaways?' To save family fights, make sure you consult everyone concerned.

If you have to say no to a request, then a simple explanation of why you are saying no (such as, 'I haven't allowed for it in our spending plan') should suffice. If your kids want to argue about your answer, ask them the question, 'Why did I just say no?' This helps them see it from your perspective, and gets them to state the reason themselves.

Remember, your decision is final. If they are particularly insistent, ask them what part of no they don't understand, and stick to your guns!

2. SET BOUNDARIES NOW AND FOR THE FUTURE

If you are going to stop your kids sending you broke, ground rules are important. Tell your kids as they are growing up what the rules are going to be about various issues – such as borrowing the car, paying board, borrowing money, dating, smoking, drinking, etc – before the actual issue arises. You will save yourself a lot of stress later on if your children have grown up knowing what the grounds rules are.

You need to anticipate questions you are going to be asked when your kids are older. It is much easier, for example, to tell a 10 year old boy, who hasn't yet begun entertaining the idea of borrowing your car, what the family rules are going to be when he gets to driving age.

You may find you and your partner have different ideas about how to parent in some situations, so it is important to discuss these issues privately before you need to enforce them.

One area that provides an excellent example for what I mean by setting boundaries is use of family vehicles. In our family we decided that driving a car was an adult activity that came with adult responsibilities. But we also wanted to encourage our children to find part time work while they were still at school and be able to drive to and from their jobs without relying on us. That meant they would need to use our vehicle.

We decided that they would have to save $500 and give it to us as a kind of bond before they could use the car. This amount would be about half of the insurance excess if they had an accident.

They also knew that if they did have a crash, they would also have to pay the remainder of the excess.

Initially, we ferried them from work as the public transport system didn't run late enough. But they both really wanted to drive themselves to their jobs at the local supermarket instead of us picking them up. So as soon as they were earning money they started saving the $500. We promised that when they had their own cars, we would give them the money back. It was an exciting day for them, and for us (albeit a bit nerve-wracking!), when they were able to drive themselves. Making them wait and showing some adult responsibility also taught them the importance of delayed gratification – often it is better to wait for what you want rather than have it immediately.

One way to let your kids send you broke is to lend them your car without any boundaries. Make sure you have them listed on your insurance policy so that they are an authorised driver of your car. Failure to do so could mean your car is uninsured when they are driving it.

We also decided, and made sure our kids knew, that if they got a speeding or parking fine while driving our car then they wouldn't be able to drive the car again until they had given us the money to pay the fine. Thankfully we never had to enforce this rule.

You may think our children sound like saints and they never did anything wrong! It's normal for kids to test the boundaries sometimes. Your job as a parent is to enforce the boundaries fairly, firmly and with lots of love. It is part of becoming a responsible adult. Our son used to like to test the boundaries sometimes. We heard via the grapevine that he had given a ride to a friend when he was on a restricted driver's licence.

We had a family discussion, and asked him if he knew what the consequences could have been if he had been stopped by the police. We also gave him some strategies so that he could say no to his friends when they were begging for a ride, so it was easier for him. We suggested he tell his friends that if his mum and dad found out he was breaking the law, he wouldn't be able to borrow the car again. He also told them our car wouldn't be insured if he broke the law.

As with most of the issues discussed in this book, it isn't just about finances, it's about effective parenting. Discuss important issues with your partner and decide what family policy is going to be. Pass those policies onto your kids before emotional and difficult situations arise. If you are a solo mum or dad then find someone who you think has done a good job of raising their kids and ask their opinion.

Here are some key issues, financial and more general, for which you might want to establish boundaries:

Borrowing the family car
Speeding fines in your car
Consequences for breaking agreements
Dating
Pubs
Sex
Lending money
Going guarantor
Language
Friends
Honesty
Caring for family
Parties
Paying board
Boyfriends / girlfriends staying the night

Alcohol
Smoking
Pocket Money
Allowance

Don't convey your policies in a heavy-handed way but as a natural part of family conversation and interaction. Establish boundaries and be sure your kids know what will be expected of them, and what their responsibility will be, as they grow into young adults and then mature adults.

Of course, your children will have opinions of their own about how things should be. Often this will be based on what their friends are allowed to do. Remember, don't be sucked in by 'but my friend's parents...'!

After our son left school, while he was still living with us, we wanted him to pay board so he didn't get such a shock when he eventually left home. We also wanted to start focusing on thinking about our own financial future. Our son used to tell us, 'But my friend's parents don't make *him* pay board.' We told our son, 'We aren't other people's parents!' But it was a policy that we had established earlier so our kids knew what to expect when the time came.

While they were still at school and had part-time jobs we didn't make them contribute to the household expenses. They used some of their income to pay for activities they wanted to do that didn't fit into our spending plan and to save for things they particularly wanted.

When our son got his first job, we discussed how much board he was going to pay out of his first week's wages. I felt a real joy at the pleased look on his face when he came to give me his first week's board and I said, 'It's okay, son, you can keep your first two weeks' wages.'

When they were young adults responsible for their own finances, we insisted on both our children paying some sort of board from any income they received, whether it came from a student allowance, a benefit or a job.

It is easier to have rules that are a bit harsh and relax them, than having wishy washy boundaries and then try to enforce something the kids weren't expecting.

3. TEACH YOUR KIDS TO LOOK AFTER THEIR STUFF

You can go broke if you continually spend money on replacing items your kids have lost or damaged because they were careless.

We all know that 'kids will be kids', and they generally aren't too concerned if they left their socks, t-shirt or towel behind somewhere, because there's another one at home.

So what's the solution? Firstly, do what you can to get back lost items. Write your child's name on everything. This also helps prevent other children from wandering off with your kids' belongings (whether by mistake or on purpose). This is essential for uniforms and stationery.

Have your kids tidy up after themselves, and when they're clearing away their toys, get them in the habit of checking that all the pieces are there. Don't just take their word for granted, check that they're right, so they know you're serious.

Don't be afraid to temporarily remove use of a certain toy or other item, such as a bike, if they don't put it away after using it.

Teach your kids to be responsible, make them pay for things themselves if they lose or break stuff. Either take them to the shops with savings from their pocket money to pay for what they have lost, or don't give them pocket money until the item has been paid for.

Sometimes accidents happen, of course. Things break accidentally, because they are poorly made. So allowances need to be made in this situation – be fair in your judgement calls.

This is another situation where ground rules are important.

Make sure your kids know what your policy is on lost or broken items. A child who is told that they will have to pay for a certain item, if it gets lost or broken, might be upset. But deep down they will know what their responsibility is. If you follow through, they will learn a great, though perhaps hard, lesson. However, if they make a mistake and lose or break an item, and you spring your policy on them suddenly, this could cause resentment. Remember, you need to follow through with making them honour their responsibilities, otherwise they will take advantage of the situation in the future, or just carry on being careless.

By the way, don't immediately fall for the 'someone has stolen it' excuse. Go check out the situation with the school. You may find that the supposedly 'stolen' item was in their desk all along!

When our kids were young, I used to earn extra money by looking after a 5-year-old, called James, after school. When his mum came to pick him up from my house after his first day, she asked him where his socks were. He couldn't find them, so she said to him, 'We'll have to buy some more. So the money will have to come out of your pocket money jar.'

James was so upset and started crying. His mum firmly and lovingly said that she had told him before that if he wanted to take off his socks at school then he would either have to put them in his shoes or put them in his jacket pocket and zip it up so they didn't get lost. He hadn't done what he was supposed to do, so he had to face the consequences.

The next day the same thing happened – no socks and more tears – but determination from Mum. She was adamant that she wasn't paying for things that got lost if he hadn't looked after them. The third day when he arrived at my house after school, he had a big smile on his face and showed me his two socks stuffed firmly down his shoes.

James's mum told me how she had taken him to the shops on the first two days and let him choose the replacement socks that he was paying for. He was saving for something special and didn't like spending his money on socks! The whole episode meant that it was going to take him longer to get what he wanted, but he had learned a great lesson.

James wasn't the only one who learnt something. From that day on, I always tried to teach my kids to look after their stuff so they didn't send me broke!

4. TEACH YOUR KIDS GOOD DECISION MAKING

Sometimes clear decision-making can be the most difficult thing to do.

Dr Edward de Bono believes that we can be taught to think more clearly and make better decisions. The following has been adapted from the website www.edwdebono.com and is used with permission.

When we are faced with an issue, we need to learn to look outside the problem as if we were helping someone else make good decisions. The decision should be based on facts, not purely on emotion. Dr de Bono explains his method through the use of six different coloured 'thinking hats' – each hat views the problem from a different angle. He suggests that you enact wearing the hats when you're learning the technique, but you could hold a different coloured pen, piece of paper etc, rather than putting on an actual hat! Here are what each of the different hats represent:

The White Hat – Asks for facts and information

What information do we have? What information do we need? What do you know about the situation? What do you need to find out? Are these true facts or opinion? Where do we get the information?

The Yellow Hat – Looks at benefits and positive points

This hat works out the 'how' and 'why' something will work and the benefits that will occur as a result of some proposed action.

The Black Hat – Caution and judgement

This is probably the most valuable of the hats as it is used to point out why a possible solution may not fit the facts. It sets off warning bells and often prevents mistakes being made. What may happen in the future? Does this fit past experience? Have I made these types of mistakes before? Can I trust my emotions? Am I asking the right people?

Green Hat – Creativity and new ideas

This hat represents the deliberate action of creating new ideas. Humour and 'thinking outside the box' come under this category. What could be a fun way I could do this? Could I adapt something else I have? Are there other people who could help me?

Red Hat – Feelings and emotions

In other words, what is my gut reaction? What do I really feel about this?

Blue Hat – The thinking process

With this hat you look back on the entire decision-making and thinking process. Have I put on each hat and looked at the situation from all angles? Is my thinking rational or irrational? What other questions could I ask? Am I asking the right questions? Am I asking the right people?

If you get into the habit of looking at situations from all angles, it is a great skill to use and to teach your children, as it applies to all areas of your life – not only money.

PART FOUR: Raise Financially Savvy Kids

We've seen that kids learn a lot by the way you run your everyday life, and by being participants in making sure the household functions smoothly. But you can also be very deliberate about educating your children in financial matters. The following chapters are about teaching your kids to be money experts who will grow into adults who don't rely on their parents.

1. TEACH THEM ABOUT MONEY

Even though this book is about how to prevent your kids sending *you* broke, it is your responsibility as a parent to train your kids and give them the necessary skills and advice to stop *them* going broke! This will help prevent you feeling like you have to rescue your kids financially if they mess up in the future. Throughout the book, I've touched on how best to teach your kids about financial issues, but now I want to recap some details and focus on others in more detail.

Discussing family financial affairs is a subject that many parents shy away from. It seems like money and sex are in the same category – discussed only when absolutely necessary (and generally too late)! In order to help put your child on the right financial path, it is vital that you (the adult) 'build a bridge and get over it'. Include your child in the financial life of your family. Usually the best way to teach your child is when they think they are not learning.

Here are some suggestions for ways you could include your child in financial matters. Show them how to pay bills online. Explain your last power bill, and how it is worked out. Show them your last bank statement and read it to them as a story of what has happened in your financial life over the past month.

Get your child to help you spend your weekly grocery allowance. This isn't about letting them buy all the stuff they want, but teaching them sensible buying that takes the needs of the family into account. Remember, if the total comes to more than the cash you have, then you need to be prepared to put some items back to demonstrate that you can't spend more than you have. When you get home, encourage your child to play detective by getting them to check every item off the docket. Offer a prize if they find an error. By taking your child back to the store with your docket and getting a refund if you have been overcharged, you will reinforce that making more money isn't always the answer – what you do with what you earn is what matters.

Eat your way out of debt

Another way to include your children in the financial life of your family is to get them on board to help you pay off any consumer debt you may have. They can be involved as you pay off such things as interest-free loans, credit cards or bills. The following true story demonstrates how you can bring your kids into the financial life of your family and teach them about borrowing and repaying.

> My friend was finding it difficult to visualise her debt in a tangible way. It was just figures on a piece of paper to her. The debts she had were holding her back in many areas of her life.
>
> I had an idea that I thought would help her. I bought some clear plastic containers and a big bag of 'Smarties' sweets. I asked her to label each container with the name of each debt, together with the amount owing and the regular payment amount. The first debt she wanted to pay off was for repairs to her washing machine. The outstanding amount was $160. Her weekly payment

was $10. I made the 'value' of each sweet $10. So $160 divided by $10 = 16 sweets, which we put into the plastic container for that debt. Then we did the same for her other debts as well.

The first time she made a payment for the washing machine repairs, she rewarded herself by eating one sweet. She decided to trim her grocery bill by $10 each week and add that amount to her repayments. This is called a 'debt acceleration amount'. So now she was paying $20 per week; reducing her debt more quickly and giving her two Smarties to eat each week! She also got her children involved – they each took a turn at eating a Smartie and helped Mum eat her way out of debt!

She paid off the first debt in just over half the projected time. Encouraged by the results she was achieving, she added the extra $20 per week she now had to the repayments of her next debt. She was now paying off that debt at $30 per week and eating three sweets a week (with help from her kids). My experiment worked a treat (if you'll excuse the pun) and she paid off a considerable amount of debt over the course of a year.

This can be a good way to visualise your debt, get rid of it as fast as possible, and give your kids a real life lesson on the realities of making repayments.

There is a misconception that schools are solely responsible for teaching your child to be financially intelligent. Some people think that because some parents aren't very good at teaching kids about money, it has to happen at school. But I think that teaching children about money has to happen at home first and be supported by the education system. Not the other way around.

My first book, *How to Stop Your Kids Going Broke* has a step by step guide with exercises which you can use to teach your kids about money.

The book uses my 'Silbo System'. The Silbo System comprises eight steps to teach parents and kids how to be – and stay – financially well. I encourage you to get hold of the book and make use of it.

The eight steps to raising financially savvy kids with a brief explanation are:

Talk

Talk to your kids about money. Bring them into the financial life of your family.

Transform – your thinking

A faulty belief system can hinder you from being and staying financially well.

Think – of others

Give to others and think about how your actions can affect other people.

Toil

Work for all you get.

Target

Have a goal to reach.

Track

Track what money comes in and what money goes out.

Trim

Look at all your expenses and trim out excess to make a spending plan balance.

Train

Train yourself how money works.

Here are some other practical areas where you can teach your children about how money works in the real world.

Think about the cost of a habit over a number of years

Recently I conducted a seminar for 18 to 25 year olds. Many of them had been smoking or drinking for a number of years. We looked at the cost of smoking over a long period of time. Most of these young adults were surprised about how much they had already spent on cigarettes or alcohol. They had never added up how much their habit had cost them so far and, if they continued to smoke, how much it would cost them over the next 20 years.

If you are a smoker, for example, take the cost of a packet of cigarettes and then multiply that by the number of packets you smoke per week. Then multiple that result by 52 to see how much your habit is costing you per year. You can do the same for other treats, luxuries and habits.

I'm not saying that you (or your kids) shouldn't have any treats. What I want you to think about is what you spend on a regular basis and work out the cost of your treats, or habits, over a long period of time. This isn't just about coffee and cigarettes! You may also need to think about the treats you are regularly buying for your children. Make sure you're informed about how these relatively small amounts add up.

A member of my extended family couldn't work out why she wasn't able to save for a house, even though she was single, had no children, and was earning a considerable income. When I suggested she keep a record of every amount she spent for a week, she discovered the true cost of one of her luxuries. She was buying a coffee on her way to work and on her way home, five days a week. Have a look at the following picture to see how this 'little' amount had added up over time.

The deposit for her house had been swallowed up by her cappuccino habit.

Contracts

Many people sign contracts without reading them thoroughly or understanding them. We are told to 'just sign here', only to find out later that the fine print contained things we should never have agreed to.

My dad always told me, 'Never sign an agreement without reading it fully and always get a copy of what you have signed.' This simple piece of advice has stuck in my head and helped to prevent me from going broke.

Think about the following scenario. You are signing a lease to rent a house. The sales person hands you the document and says, 'Just sign here, it's a standard contract we use.' You duly make your mark on the dotted line. Now, as we have discussed, children are sponges. If your child was watching what just happened, think about what they learned without you saying a word – that it's okay to sign a contract without reading it. When they grow up they will model what you did.

Remember, kids can learn poor financial principles from you without you saying a word.

> During one of my seminars, 'Eight Steps to Raising Financially Savvy Kids', one parent told me that he had been signing his child's homework book without even looking at what he was signing. After hearing what I had to say, he was determined that he was going to stop doing this. He realised that he was potentially setting up his child to carelessly sign things in the future. He was able to imagine devastating consequences and the

feeling of guilt he would experience if his child unwisely committed to something because of the behaviour he himself had modelled.

The cost of buying cars with finance

As a former budget advisor, I think some of the saddest stories I heard were when things went wrong with car finance. Hopefully the global financial meltdown has changed the behaviour of lending companies, but over the last decade a vast amount of money was loaned to people who really couldn't afford the repayments. For many people, it came down to a choice between meeting repayments or having food on the table. Parents, please, please, please educate your kids about the real cost of buying cars with finance.

The story below demonstrates the true cost of buying a car with finance. These figures are taken from a real finance contract shown to me by one of my former clients; let's call her Jill.

Jill bought a car by trading in her old vehicle and getting finance to pay for the rest. Two years later, it broke down. She wasn't worried as she had taken out Mechanical Breakdown Insurance when she purchased the vehicle. However, she had failed to read the fine print, which stipulated that the vehicle had to be serviced regularly by a qualified mechanic. She failed to meet that criteria, and on that basis her insurance claim was rejected. So, now she still had to pay her weekly loan repayment of around $70, but was unable to drive the vehicle as she couldn't afford the repairs.

The situation was very stressful as Jill was a solo mum with a new baby and two other children. However, she was able to get some help through her local church to get the car fixed.

When she finally finished paying off the loan, she had the car valued. The most she could get for it was $3000, so she decided to keep the vehicle as she didn't think it was worth selling. One year later, the car again broke down and the motor was beyond repair. She eventually sold the car for parts and was given $500.

Car advertised for sale	$7,990
Payment Insurance	$405
Mechanical Breakdown Insurance	$760
Statutory Fees	$3
Comprehensive Insurance	$995
	$10,153

Cost of car	$10,153
Trade In	$2,000
Total to be borrowed	$8,153

4 years later...

AT 19% INTEREST PER ANNUM

Total to be borrowed	$8,153
Booking Fee	$350
Total interest charged	$4,135.45

$12,638.46!!

TOTAL COST TO PURCHASE THE CAR

She had started off this nightmare process with a debt-free vehicle worth $2000. After she had used this as a trade-in, she ended up paying nearly $13,000 for the new car on finance. Five years after taking possession of the vehicle, she sold it for $500. The whole situation had resulted in a terrible financial loss.

Consolidating debt

When things get really tight, some people fall into the trap of consolidating their debt. Finance companies and banks put a lot of effort into marketing 'debt consolidation loans' and it can seem like an attractive option. But be careful of consolidating all your debts into one loan, as it can cost you a lot more in interest in the long run. I can't stress this enough. Be very careful about taking out a loan to consolidate debts, especially when the company wants to take out a secured loan against your car or house. I have witnessed people having to sell their home or car because 'easy weekly payments' turned into a massive debt burden.

If you haven't done a spending and savings plan and improved your financial habits, you can end up seeking loan after loan to cover yourself. Eventually you can be swamped by debt.

Understanding the big picture of financial health

By teaching your children how money works in the real world, they can begin to understand how financial decisions will impact their lives. Have a look at the illustration on the following page.

HEALTHY TREE

FRUITS

1 Never in overdraft
2 Have money for unexpected expenses
3 No credit card interest
4 Have money put aside for bills
5 Spare money for investing
6 Not paying any interest on 'stuff' on HP
7 Know exactly where my money goes
8 Able to achieve my financial goals
9 Receiving passive income
10 Have contracts that I understand

SICK TREE

FRUITS

1 Always owing money
2 No money for unexpected expenses
3 Paying credit card interest
4 No money for bills
5 Unable to do any investing
6 Paying interest on 'stuff' on HP
7 No idea where my money goes
8 No control over my financial future
9 No assets producing income
10 Locked into bad contracts

HEALTHY TREE – ROOTS

1 Spend less than I earn
2 Save 10% of income
3 Credit card paid off in full
4 Have a spending and savings plan
5 Don'y buy unnecessary 'wants'
6 Don't put things on hire purchase
7 Always track where my money goes
8 Have SMART money goals
9 Own assets that produce passive income
10 Always read contracts before signing

SICK TREE – ROOTS

1 Spend more than I earn
2 Don't save any of my income
3 Don't pay off my credit cards
4 No spending plan for expenses
5 Spend on unnecessary 'wants'
6 Have things on hire purchase
7 Don't track where my money goes
8 No financial goals
9 Own no income producing assets
10 Never read contracts before signing

To change the FRUITS (visible) you have to change the ROOTS (invisible)

On the left side, the tree has healthy foliage and deep roots. But the tree on the right looks like it is dying. It has hardly any leaves and shallow roots. These two views of the tree show the consequences of wise and unwise money management. Help your kids grow a healthy tree!

2. USE CASH TO TEACH THEM MONEY SKILLS

From a very early age (even as young as two), children can start to get the idea of a spending plan.

Having your children learn the simple concept of 'telling their money where to go', instead of wondering where it's gone, helps create a great habit that teaches effective money management. It is important for your child to actually handle money to see how it feels, to see it build up and what it feels like when it is all spent.

When you give your kids money, use cash (I'll discuss pocket money and allowances in the next two chapters). Have them put the money into three containers labelled 'spending', 'savings' and 'sharing', so they learn that every dollar they get has a job.

The terms 'spending' and 'saving' are probably self-explanatory. But the concept of a 'sharing' jar is a little more unusual. I believe that giving money away to community organisations or charities is a tremendously positive thing, and it's a principle you can teach your kids. Through it, children learn to think of others and be generous. Teach them to share (give away) some of what they get. This helps your kids to have a mindset of thankfulness rather than one of entitlement. Help your child choose a charitable organisation and let them get excited about the amazing work that organisation does.

Your kind deed of regularly transferring money into a savings account for your children, if that's what you do, does nothing to teach them about handling money. Seeing the money build up in their jars, and taking it out to count, gives a child the concept that money is a real thing, and doesn't just exist inside a magic plastic card. Once a certain goal has been reached, take them along to the bank and deposit their savings into an account. This teaches them about money in a tangible way and demonstrates that money belongs in the bank. If your school has school banking, then your kids can bank their money that way.

If your children want to spend some money from their savings jar, then when it's gone, it's gone. Don't give them a bit extra because they don't have enough. If they want something that is 10 cents more than they have, make them wait until next week when they have some more pocket money.

Remember, be careful not to rescue your child if they have spent all their money from their spending or savings jar and want to buy something else. Letting your child borrow from you until next pay day is teaching them to spend more than they have. This can have serious consequences in the future when they are old enough to take out loans.

When I was a young child, I was given a certain amount of cash just before Christmas so that I could buy presents for my family. I am one of seven children and I became an aunty when I was seven years old, so there were lots of people to buy presents for.

I can still remember the joy of sitting down to write out a list of the presents I would need. Being fairly generous by nature, I wrote on my list each of my five brothers, my sister, Mum, Dad, my teacher, one surviving grandparent, two nieces, one nephew, my two best friends, my piano teacher, plus neighbours. It was quite a list!

I can't remember the exact figures, because it was a long time ago, but I do remember the essence of what I was taught and the thrill of going out with the cash and my list.

Let's say I was given today's equivalent of about $20. Mum had me add up how many people I wanted to buy for, which came to 18 people. When we divided 18 into $20, I discovered that I had just $1.11 for each person. I informed my mother that this wouldn't be enough, and that I would need more money from her. Mum said I had some choices to make, as that was the amount she had budgeted to give me. I could take some people off my list, find a way of earning some extra money myself, or make something for people using the resources we had at home – such as flour for making biscuits.

I didn't want to take anyone off the list, so I decided to buy presents for my mum and dad, Grandma and my two nieces and one nephew. Mum helped me make biscuits so that I had gifts to give to the rest of my family. So now my $20 was divided by six people so I had $3.33 to spend on each person. I used wrapping paper which Mum had saved from other presents she had received and I made cards instead of buying them.

As part of our work providing books to school libraries, my husband and I have managed to stay in touch with modern parents, even though our own children are now grown up. I'm often inspired by the stories parents tell me about how they teach their kids the value of money and how to manage resources. Here are two stories that I've heard recently...

In one family, the children were given the job of creating a natural disaster survival plan. This plan needed to provide for the whole family for three days, and included buying suitable food, allowing for a cooking method and other needs such as lighting and water storage. Then, to test the plan during the school holidays, the family lived for three days without any modern conveniences (including water from the tap) using the survival kit the children had put together. (The only exception to the conditions was that the family was allowed to use the toilet.) They soon found that they didn't have quite enough healthy snacks or drinking water! But by doing this exercise, the kids learnt how to use resources wisely.

Another family has a tradition that when a child turns 10, he or she is given $300 to fund a trip away for the whole family (Mum and Dad and the four kids) for a weekend. The parents take care of petrol costs, but the child chooses how to use the money to pay for food and accommodation. Certain boundaries are provided; for example, the food can't just be a whole lot of chips – it had to be nutritious. At the time when the mother of the family told me this story, two of her children had already met the challenge. Her third child, who had just had his tenth birthday, was waiting for the weather to improve as he wanted to take the family on a trip to the beach.

If you're short of ideas on how to teach your kids about money, ask other parents. You never know, you may start a craze of helping kids have fun while they learn how money works!

Recently my husband and I were at a training seminar run by Christians Against Poverty. The following story was read out to illustrate the power of teaching children (even very young children) what to do with money when they get it. It further illustrates the value of raising financially savvy kids.

> Our son Kane is two. He doesn't get 'official' pocket money, but he's pretty good at finding a jingly pocket on a grandparent or uncle... he's showing a real talent for fundraising! He occasionally gets a coin for doing something really helpful too, so he might be given two or three dollars all together over the course of a week.
>
> We really want him to grow up with sound money skills. We've had to learn a lot of things the hard way in our own lives and we'd love to see good financial sense be a part of his thinking all through his life (rather than a mad catch-up in his late 20s).
>
> Toddlers really need things to be visual and short-term, so we split his money into three jars that live on a shelf where he can see them and deal with his finances on a weekly basis.
>
> Jar one is for giving. We try to encourage him to be generous. Sometimes he gives it to the guy that busks for the RSA at the market, or the Salvation Army collectors, sometimes the collection at church – we let him choose.

Jar two is for saving. We bank it when he's accumulated a bit. The concept of 'the bank' is really too abstract for him to grasp at the moment, but we're hoping to form a habit anyway and he'll understand eventually.

Jar three is for spending (usually on a lamb kebab at the Saturday market!). In the future (when he discovers Lego) we'll show him how to save up the 'spend' portion of his money for bigger purchases.

We try to keep it low-key and fun, and also small-coin-based: paper money or even a $2 coin is not nearly as interesting to a toddler as a handful of 10c pieces! It also needs to be hands-on – we let him handle the money directly.

We've got a long way to go but hopefully this is a start!

Kane is now four years old and his mum provided this update:

Having used this budgeting method for around two years now, it's second nature for Kane to put any money he gets into his jars and think about how to distribute it. To be honest, I did used to wonder if he was too young to understand, but it's become a habit anyway and he's beginning to appreciate the reasons behind what we do. I hope it's still second nature to him when he's earning real money – he'll find money management a lot easier than his dad and I do! We didn't have any positive financial role models growing up, so we want to give him a head-start in life.

3. GIVE POCKET MONEY

As I said in the previous chapter, it is a great idea to let your children handle money from an early age. For kids under 12, giving them pocket money is the best way.

Pros and cons of pocket money

There are many different views on whether children should or shouldn't get pocket money.

There are also different views as to whether they should be required to work for their pocket money or be given it as a gift with nothing required in return.

Parents may choose to pay their children an amount per week that is linked to doing certain routine household jobs. If these jobs aren't completed, then money is deducted. If extra jobs are done, extra money is added.

Let's examine the pros and cons of having children work for their pocket money or being given it with no strings attached.

Working for pocket money

One of the benefits of getting kids to work for their pocket money is that they can learn that work = money. No work = no pay. The more work you do = the more money you get.

However, the human mind is a complicated thing! It interprets experiences in different ways. Some children brought up in an environment where they worked for their pocket money will assume that they should always be paid for doing jobs around the home. The concept of doing jobs around the home voluntarily, or because it is the right thing to do, doesn't enter into their head. When they are teenagers, or even earlier, it can cause friction when you ask them to do something for you and they reply, 'How much are you going to pay me?' However a mature adult knows that there are lots of things that need doing in life, regardless of whether there is a direct pay-off.

Parents should also consider that if kids think they are working for the money, then they also often think that they should be able to spend it how they like, so can be grumpy when told what to do with the money they have earned. This can stand in the way of you instructing them in creating a savings plan, for example.

Not working for pocket money

The good thing about giving children pocket money that isn't connected to the jobs they do around the house, is that it can counteract some of the negative side effects that we discussed above. It also gives them a sum of money that can be used to teach them budgeting skills as we saw earlier.

The downside of this approach is that it could potentially result in them having an attitude of 'entitlement' that encourages them to expect a hand-out. They could grow up expecting that they will never have to work for money, and as the old saying goes, 'Easy come, easy go.' It is often easier to spend unwisely if you haven't had to earn the money first.

Which option?

In my opinion, I think it is best to teach children that in the home they are part of the family team. There are things like making their beds, doing dishes, taking out the rubbish, cooking a meal, or cleaning the bathroom basin, that are done because it helps make their family team function well. There is no payment attached. They do it because it is the right thing to do. It also teaches them valuable skills for when the inevitable happens and they leave home.

Additional money can be earned at home such as washing your car or painting the house. In other words, payment can be given for jobs that are not part of the normal daily family routine.

Better still, get them earning their own money outside the home. I'll discuss that in the following chapters.

How you administer pocket money is a matter for you to decide. Talk to your children to help counteract some of the potential negative side effects of your pocket money policy. But whatever pocket money system you choose, be conscious of the long term benefits or negative effects this could have on your children (and on you).

4. GIVE AN ALLOWANCE

If you feel your kids are sending you broke because they are continually asking for things, and you don't like to say no because you are a bit of a soft touch, then giving them an allowance when they become teenagers can be the answer for you. We did this with our children and found it to be incredibly freeing. Whenever our kids came to us with a request for something they wanted, we were able to say, 'Sure you can, if you pay for it yourself out of your allowance.'

Here's how it worked. When they were about 12 years old, we gave our children an allowance which we paid each month. We sat down with them and worked out everything we spent on them over the year for things such as fast food, movies, clothes, outings, money for them to buy gifts (for us, their friends and relations) and giving to charity. We then divided the total amount by 12 to get a monthly amount; that was their allowance. We also made sure the allowance amount was in keeping with our household spending plan. We didn't end up spending any more on them, we just diverted into their allowances what we had already been spending.

We continued to pay school-related costs, medical costs and all costs associated with family outings. For example, if we went on a family outing to the movies and we decided to buy our lunch instead of taking it from home, then we would pay for the lunch. However, if our kids were going out with their friends, and asked for money to buy some lunch while they were out, then the answer was 'No – that's what your allowance is for.' They had the choice of either taking something from home for lunch or buying it themselves out of their allowance.

To make it crystal clear who was responsible for what, we wrote a list. We made a simple contract, and we all signed it. One of the conditions associated with their allowances was that they had to keep a record of their spending on a spreadsheet. I have to admit that this wasn't totally successful as our son could never get his to balance! But at least it gave him the idea of tracking his spending.

These days, with modern technology, the tracking part is a lot easier. There are many software packages that can help you keep track of your money – look for a 'freeware' one on the internet. I particularly like and use a free product which has been designed by a Kiwi. You can download it at www.acclaim.co.nz.

When we first set up the allowance, my husband and I were both working, so we were able to be quite generous. A year after starting our kids on allowances, I decided I wanted to study. Then, virtually a week after I enrolled and was ready to begin, my husband's job was unexpectedly made redundant.

So it was back to the drawing board! We sat down again and went through our budget. Unfortunately figures don't lie. We were forced to cut our kids' allowances in half. All of us now had to learn to live with less income. Buying clothes from opportunity shops and buying less fast foods became the norm. The kids rallied, and a part time job delivering brochures all of a sudden became more appealing than when we had suggested it earlier!

When our kids first started getting an allowance they thought they were going to be very rich one day.

However, when our daughter spent nearly her entire monthly allowance on one piece of clothing, she had to face the fact that she didn't have enough money to go to the movies with her friends. It was hard for us as parents to resist the temptation to rescue her by advancing her some money from the next allowance. These kinds of lessons help prepare a person for their future. I am proud to say our children (now adults), though not yet on New Zealand's 'Rich List', both handle money responsibly and have no consumer debt. I have had to chuckle on the odd occasion when both our kids have bought their friends to me and said something along the lines of, 'Mum, show them how to budget, they don't have any idea.'

As children become older and show responsibility, then extra money can be added to their allowance to pay for just about everything that an adult has to pay for in the real world.

5. GET YOUR KIDS EARNING THEIR OWN MONEY

One day, when I was visiting my parents-in-law, I noticed two kids from a nearby house who had set up a roadside stall selling lemonade by the glassful. My father-in-law also told me about a young boy who had come to the door recently, trying to sell a good sized fish he has just caught. I think it's wonderful to see kids thinking about how they can earn their own money. Kids like that are less likely to be KIPPERS or send their parents broke.

The human mind has a great capacity for creativity. Think of all the technology in the world that we take for granted – they all exist because somebody, somewhere, had an idea.

When it comes to earning money, it can help to bring some of that amazing creativity to the situation. Sometimes ideas come naturally and other times it helps to brainstorm with your kids and their friend's kids to help get the creative juices flowing. There are lots of possibilities – some are obvious, some less so.

Tell your kids about the types of things you did as a child to earn money. For example, my husband used to collect pine cones and bag them to sell to people for firewood. You could also look on the internet for ideas for ways for kids to earn money or check the local library.

Get a large piece of paper and write down all the money-earning ideas that the family comes up with. Get your kids to ask their friends, grandparents, aunts, uncles, etc, for ideas as well.

Helping your child with financial creative thinking and brainstorming could be the making of a budding entrepreneur.

If they are earning their own money, there is very little chance that your kids will send you broke. You never know, you may awaken a financial genius in them! They may go on to support you in your old age or become philanthropists who have a desire to improve the material, social, and spiritual welfare of humanity. It's a possibility!

We had a huge plum tree growing in our back yard when our children were young. We suggested they bag the plums and sell them. We told the kids to ring up the local supermarket to enquire about the current price of plums, and then offer the fruit for half that price to people in our street. For safety, we made sure they went out in twos.

Our son and his friend, and our daughter and her friend, decided to have a competition to see who could sell the most plums. The girls bagged their portion of the fruit into one kilogram bags and sold them by the kilo, whereas the boys just put their fruit in bags of random weights and sizes. Then they all went out door-knocking in the neighbourhood. The girls won, as people liked to know how many plums they were getting for their money. But at the end of the day, the kids learned that money could be made with a little bit of effort and creative thinking.

Work ethic

In order for your kids to become financially independent, they need to develop a great work ethic. They need a great work ethic whether they are working for themselves or for someone else.

Ensuring kids do the jobs that are assigned to them at home is a good way to teach work ethics, such as turning up on time, finishing what they start and doing everything to the best of their abilities.

Your role as a parent is to guide them so that they know that, in most cases, work = money.

I say, 'in most cases', because it is also a wonderful thing to teach your kids about giving up their working time for free.

For example, getting your kids to mow an elderly neighbours' lawn for free can be a great way for your child to learn some skills (such as mowing the lawn) and to get used to working regularly for someone outside the home. But more importantly, it teaches them to think of others. A person who thinks of others is a great person to have around in your family and in society in general.

While volunteering doesn't create immediate income, it can have a financial pay-off. Your child will be nearer the top of the pile when employers are looking for staff. Often, a good *attitude* is more desirable than brilliant *aptitude*. I would much rather employ a young adult who has a great attitude and is willing to learn, than one who is brilliant academically but who has an attitude of entitlement.

6. TEACH THEM TO SAVE FOR THEIR OWN FUTURE

Some parents encourage their children to save up for a specific item that the child wants to buy. This is a useful skill to teach your kids, but mostly it involves saving towards short term financial goals – such as buying a game for their Xbox, a new bike, a toy, an iPod or a cellphone. When they reach their goal, they empty their bank account and start saving towards the next thing they want to buy.

Although this habit is much smarter than buying things on hire purchase and paying interest, it does nothing about saving towards long-term financial goals such as studying, buying a car, buying a house or providing for retirement.

When budget advising, I noticed that the purchase of a car and taking on a student loan are usually a young adult's first major financial commitments. With some forward thinking though, borrowing for these things can be prevented or greatly reduced.

When a child is about 12 years old, you can do this exercise with them (there is no specific age, but the sooner the better): Discuss the cost of a vehicle with your child. Show them the listings on TradeMe and at car dealerships. Also talk about the cost of insurance, registration, warrants of fitness, petrol and repairs.

Find a car your child likes, and then together pretend that your child is going to buy it with finance. Work out how much the car will end up costing with interest and fees added. Then do the same exercise, but this time pretend your child is going to save up for the car and pay cash. Make sure you include saving one year's insurance costs, registration and the warrant of fitness as well. Show them the difference in the total cost between buying with finance and paying with cash. That's the first thing your child can learn from this exercise.

Next you can teach them about saving. Work out how much your child would have to save until they are ready to buy a car when they are about 17 years old.

If they chose a car worth $3,000 then add $1,000 (for insurance, registration etc). That means they would have to save $4,000. From 12 years old to 17 years old is five years. Five years x 52 weeks is 260 weeks – the time available for them to save for the vehicle. Your 12 year old would need to save $15.38 each week until they are 17 years old to buy a car worth $3,000 and be able to insure and register it for a year. Many kids will want to start saving right away!

I suggest having two savings accounts to help keep kids focused on saving for the future.– one for short term goals (under a year) and one for longer term goals (over a year). It might be a challenge for a 12 year old to save $15.38 per week, but the point of the exercise is to get you and your child planning and saving for the future instead of only saving for short term goals.

Financial goal-setting

When I am setting financial goals for myself, I set them under the following headings:

Super Short Time	(under a month)
Short Time	(two years or less)
Medium Time	(five years or less)
Long Time	(ten years or less)

Long Long Time (20 years or more)

I live by the motto, 'You can't change the past, but you can design the future.' So if I am unsuccessful at reaching a goal I set, I simply reset the goal with a different timeframe.

If you are new to goal-setting, start with some simple exercises – nothing too complicated and something you know can be achieved within a week.

Make your goals **SMART** goals (Specific, Measurable, Achievable, Realistic and Timely). For example for a super short term goal, decide on an amount you are going to spend on groceries for that week – write it down – stick to it – tick it off.

With all the advertising around about 'buy now, pay later' the concept of delayed gratification has been lost from our society. The act of setting a financial goal, and waiting until the goal is reached can be a step to breaking this mindset. You really will be better off if you can be patient with your finances.

At one of my groups where I taught parents and kids how to become financially savvy, I asked for a volunteer I could work with to show an example of goal setting, using a SMART goal.

One 12-year-old told me boldly that his goal was to get a drum kit by Christmas. It was early June. He was going to save all his pocket money to get the drums and he was adamant he would achieve his goal. This young lad had been taught the concept of 'positive thinking' – just keep saying you are going to get it, and it will happen.

This is fine as far as it goes, but positive thinking alone won't get you anywhere. You need to set a goal and then put your plan into action.

We got out a huge piece of paper so the whole class could see. I asked him to be specific about his goal. He said he wanted a set of drums. I asked him to be even more specific, so he said, 'I want to buy a set of blue drums, that cost $520 and have them by Christmas time.'

Now the test: is the goal specific, measurable, attainable, realistic and timely (SMART)?

Is the goal specific? Just about. He wanted to buy a set of blue drums, which cost $520 and buy them by Christmas time. But let's say, 'Buy them by December 24' – that's even more specific.

Is the goal measurable? Yes. He knows how much he has to save and he will know when he has the drums.

Is the goal attainable? Yes, there are blue drum kits available for around that price.

And now for the last two: is the goal realistic in the time frame specified? Here's where the rubber meets the road.

I asked him how he was going to pay for the drums. He said he was going to save all his pocket money at $2 per week. I got out a calendar and we counted the weeks between June 1 and December 24, which was 29 weeks. 29 weeks x $2 per week = $58. I asked what other money he might be getting before Christmas. 'My birthday money,' he said, 'I usually get about $50.' So that meant he could have $108 by Christmas Eve. He would be short by $412.

I told him that to make this goal realistic we would have to change the timeframe. Let's see what would make it a realistic goal.

I got him to work out that at his current rate of savings, it would be another 206 weeks before he could reach his goal (nearly four years). He would be nearly 16 years old when he got his drums.

I felt so sorry for this young boy; the colour drained out of his face as he discovered that, given the current situation, his goal was not realistic. *My* goal wasn't to dash a child's dreams or deflate his ego. When we are discussing these kinds of things with our kids, we need to explain reality but offer them positive and proactive ways that they can achieve their goals. So that's where the next bit came in...

I asked him, 'How much money do you have saved now?' He told me that he had $100 saved. That meant a six-month reduction in the time he would have to wait. We were down to three and a half years.

Then I asked him if he had thought of ways he could earn money. Did he have grandparents that needed jobs doing, or neighbours whose cars he could wash? If you don't want to change the timeframe of your goal, then you need to find a way of earning extra money.

Some months later, he reported back to me. He had reached his goal! His grandparents, who owned a farm, employed him to rear calves and do jobs around the property. He let people know about his goal, and soon he found all kinds of ways to earn money. His parents helped too. When the family was out and his mum or dad offered to buy him an ice cream or something else, he would ask for the money instead and add it to his savings.

He reached his goal because he set his mind to it and put some action into achieving his dream.

PART FIVE: Let Your Kids Grow Up!

Your kids are getting into their late teenage years, finishing high school, and pretty soon they'll head out into the big wide world to start independent lives – well, that's the theory. Right from a young age, you can be preparing your children for the day they start out on their own. When they leave home, their financial savvy is going to be tested. The question is, will they come to you to bail them out; and if they do, what happens next?

1. PREPARE YOUR KIDS TO LEAVE THE NEST

How can you train up your children for the big wide world, to love them, and then let them go? How can we stop them making financial mistakes that leave them broke and, in some cases, send us broke as well?

As Benjamin Franklin said, the only certainties in life are death and taxes. So nothing you do can have a perfectly predictable outcome. Why is this? Because adults have a free choice to choose how they live their lives. As a life coach and counsellor, I have seen the negative effects of parents refusing to realise that their children are now young adults who need to be made responsible for their own actions.

Home is the training ground for a child's future. It is worth teaching your kids that when they are doing adult things, then they should take responsibility as an adult would. From an early age, kids can get a shock when the world doesn't bend its rules to suit them!

A functioning healthy adult takes full financial, physical and emotional responsibility for him or herself. Your children will always be your children but **they will not always *be* children**, and it is important to be clear about the difference.

Yvonne Godfrey is an authority on the development and behaviour of youth as they transition into adult life. She has observed that many young adults do not have the skills to successfully live independently of their parents. Unfortunately this is because these children have often been 'spoon fed'. Yvonne has identified seven key factors that allow a person to function successfully as an adult:

1. Discover personal values and strengths
2. Learn to set and achieve goals
3. Take responsibility to create pride, ownership, and contribution
4. Make decisions and solve problems
5. Master money
6. Build healthy relationships
7. Communicate clearly, honestly and effectively

Take each of these seven key areas and apply them to your family situation. How are you encouraging your child to move from being dependent to independent? Ask yourself the question, 'Am I encouraging my child to...?' for each of the seven points above. The goal is that one day they will be able to live their lives independently from you.

Are you training your children to leave home and live independently? Do they know how to cook, clean, set goals, problem solve and manage their finances? Do they know what is involved in renting a place or flatting? The alternative is that they go out into the big wide world with no skills and potentially fall flat on their faces.

Be very practical with how you teach them about life. For example, show them your latest power bill, not just the amount owing. Go through it line by line, explaining things such as customer numbers, daily fixed charges, costs per kilowatt and prompt payment discounts. Work out a set of questions to ask different power companies to ascertain if your family is getting the best deal. Then encourage older children to phone different power companies to compare prices. On your list of questions, make sure they ask if the price they are being quoted is based on having a contract for a fixed period of time.

Show your children your phone bill and discuss how much each call is costing. You can then also use this as an opportunity to talk about how you can reduce your phone costs. Again, it might be a chance to get your children calling different phone providers to compare prices.

Talk with your child about some good or bad financial decisions you have made, such as investments or asset purchases that gained value and did really well (or not so well) – let them learn from your experiences.

The main thing, as we have seen, is to include your children in the general financial life of your family so they can start to understand the 'real world' in a safe environment.

They need to understand the cost of living. Sound financial habits can be established from an early age. For example, if a child has been saving their own money throughout their lives, they will much more easily transition into the adult world and be able to take full financial responsibility for themselves. It is a real boost to their self-confidence if your young adult is able to set up house or flat for the first time without financial help from you.

There are considerable costs involved in renting a home or flat for the first time. Such things as bond, letting fee and rent in advance need to be taken into account. Then there are things to consider such as putting on the power and telephone which may require bonds too. It can cost over $1000 just to get yourself in the front door.

One area which confuses some people is the term 'rent in advance'. Some people think they are up to date with their rent, when in fact they are behind.

Paying rent in advance is best explained by using the analogy of the difference between taking a bus ride or a taxi ride. When you catch a bus, you climb aboard and give the driver your money before you go on the ride. Whereas, when you hire a taxi, you take the ride and then pay at the other end. Paying rent in advance is like getting on a week-long bus ride – you pay at the beginning of your week-long journey, then you have to pay for the next week before you ride again.

If, for example, you pay your rent every week on a Monday and you are required to be one week in advance, then when the next Monday comes around, your rent is in arrears unless you pay it.

Warn your kids about these costs so that they are prepared, and so you don't have to pay their bills for them!

Even though I am a strong advocate of encouraging your young adult to make it on their own, I do think it is great if parents are able to help out with stuff such as sheets, towels, crockery, and cutlery. Perhaps you could let them take the furniture they had at home. It could be a good time for you to have a clean out and give your kids a few items you have around the house.

This isn't about kicking your kids out and saying, 'See ya later!' It's about helping them transition into being fully-functioning and self-sufficient adults, so that you can rest easy knowing that you have given them the skills that will help protect their – and your – financial future.

2. DON'T RESCUE THEM

'Learning by experience often is painful. The more it hurts, the more you learn.' – Ralph Banks

If you see your adult kids sinking in debt and you are able to do something about it, it can be very tempting to want to rescue them, especially if there are grandchildren involved.

There are times when a *hand up* can be helpful, but a *hand out* does nothing to encourage your children to become problem solvers.

If you have taught your kids good financial principles and they have ended up in a financial pickle because of poor decisions, they will learn far more from the experience if you let them work through it themselves. As hard as it can be to watch your children go through difficulties, they will come out stronger and more independent if they take responsibility for the situation themselves. That's not to say you can't offer advice or have input into their financial strategies – just don't bail them out financially.

On the other hand, if you haven't trained them in sound financial principles (like 'spend less than you earn'), your situation will be a bit more sticky.

When I was training to be a counsellor, I learnt about a theory called the 'Karpman Triangle' which relates to how people react in certain situations. People take on different 'roles' in their lives. They 'play' either a victim, a rescuer or a persecutor role, and these roles can shift around depending on the situation. As I started coaching people, I noticed how these roles apply to situations involving personal finances.

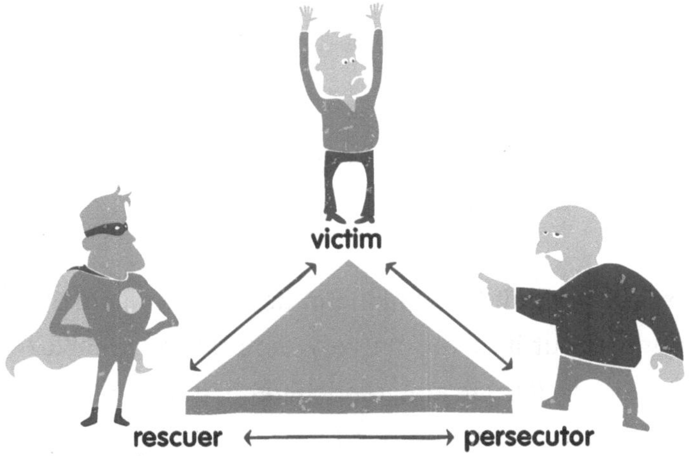

The 'victim' and the 'rescuer' type personalities are at the opposite corners of the triangle. They are often found together in relationships. These relationships function, to an extent, until the person playing 'victim' or the person playing 'rescuer' decides not to play the game anymore.

The victim tends to blame others, lives in the past, is financially irresponsible, wants to be rescued, is addictive and feels powerless. Whereas the rescuer loves to rescue, goes guarantor and bails others out. For the victim's mentality to change, he or she must realise it is their own responsibility to stay financially well. A rescuer needs to recognise that by continually coming to the rescue, he or she is perhaps preventing the victim from making this realisation.

When a rescuer decides to stop rescuing, a victim can sometimes take on the role of persecutor, using such things as emotional pressure and pestering, in an attempt to persuade the other person to resume their rescuing role.

It is great if you can help your child out occasionally when they genuinely need it. But if you continually rescue your child, or adult child, (especially if they are continually getting *themselves* into debt and making poor choices) you are not helping them to accept personal responsibility.

A hand up is better than a hand out

Here's an example of what I mean by a 'hand up'.

It's the dreaded phone call... Our teenage daughter, who is at Teachers' College in a town an hour away from home, has crashed her car, tail-ending another vehicle. Thankfully she's okay, but the vehicles weren't so lucky. Her car is covered by third party insurance – in other words, the insurance company will pay for the repairs on the other vehicle, but not hers. And because of her age, she has to pay an excess of $1500. Her car has been towed to a panel beater, who will charge her $150 for every week it is kept in his yard. The cost to repair the vehicle is estimated to be around $3000 which, of course, she doesn't have because she is a student.

My husband and I were faced with a dilemma. Give our daughter a hand out and completely pay for the repair and excess? Or give her a hand up?

We had always had the philosophy that when you are doing adult things (such as owning and driving a car), you have to take the adult responsibility that comes with them. But our hearts went out to our daughter. She was a sensible girl and she was pursuing her life's dream of becoming a primary school teacher. Despite the risks of establishing a rescuing pattern in our relationship with her, we decided to give her a hand up, dealing with the situation wisely so that she could use it to grow and mature, rather than become dependent.

First, we offered to tow the car to our house to avoid the yard fees the panel beater was going to charge. From there we would get the car assessed to see if it would be better economic value to sell the vehicle damaged, or to get it repaired and then sell it to pay for the repair work.

My husband helped our daughter obtain quotes and helped her find out what the car would be worth once it was fixed.

It was decided that my husband and I would cover the cost of repairs for now (as the vehicle was worth more fixed than damaged, even taking the cost of the repairs into consideration). Of course our daughter was very upset (and so was I) that her beloved car would need to be sold when it was repaired. We needed to recoup the repair costs and the $1500 excess still needed to be paid.

The car was repaired, and sold for $1000 more than the cost of the repairs. After paying $1000 to the insurance company, our daughter still had $500 left to pay. A few weeks later, she received a letter from the insurance company demanding full payment of the $500 by a certain date, or risk having the debt handed over to a collection agency.

As a budget advisor, I was well aware of the seriousness of a damaged credit rating. I also wanted our daughter to learn the lesson of how hard it is to pay off debt. Realistically though, she was a student earning $50 per week from part time work.

Wanting to give her another hand up, I offered to ring the insurance company on her behalf and negotiate for the debt to be paid off at a reasonable weekly amount. But I asked her to listen to the phone conversation so that she could learn negotiation skills. I knew from previous experience that these companies can be tough, so it was better for me to ring than her.

I negotiated for her to pay off her debt at $20 per week, with no interest. She was horrified when I told her it was going to take nearly six months to pay off the $500 at that rate.

She was not a happy chappy! She had no car, had to rely on public transport, and still had a debt to pay to the insurance company for a car she didn't own any more.

I helped her set up an automatic payment from her bank account to the insurance company. About two months later, the summer holidays came around and she got a full time job. I told her it was important to pay off debt before she spent her money on luxuries.

At my suggestion, she rang the insurance company to see how much she still owed. Afterwards she told me, 'The guy on the phone was so nice, Mum. He said if I could pay $200 by the end of next week, he would wipe

$150 off the debt.' She met that goal and was rewarded with a reduction of $150.

About eight years later, I find it interesting to look back and think about how we handled that situation, and why we did what we did. We could have paid outright for our daughter's car to be repaired (we had the cash at the time). But I had counselled parents who had continually rescued their kids by paying speeding fines etc, and had seen the damage that could be done.

Many of those relationships had fallen into the victim-rescuer-persecutor pattern. Often, when the parents decided to stop rescuing their child, that child would become the persecutor, blaming the parents for the financial woes he or she now found themselves in. Most times, the child was ungrateful for the help their parents had given them in the past, and were bitter that the rescuing had now stopped.

Here's an example of a 'hand out':

When I was telling a friend of mine the story of what we did when our daughter crashed her car, she told me she used to drive to and from school in a car her dad gave her. One day she had a crash. Thankfully, just the car and her pride were hurt. Her dad paid for everything to be fixed and got her another car to drive. She told me that even though it didn't cost her financially, he continually reminded her about how he had given her a car and how much it had cost him to get it repaired. Her family also constantly teased her for being a bad driver. Her dad didn't let her off the hook emotionally until one day he crashed his own car! She said that, in hindsight, it would have been easier if her dad had made her accept some responsibility financially, instead of bringing up the subject for years to come and never letting her forget what he had done.

I find it interesting to reflect back on my own childhood and see the times when my parents gave me a hand up without rescuing me.

When I was 14, my mum gave me a weekly allowance. It was agreed that my allowance would cover my bus fare to school, stockings, clothes, shoes and extra treats (such as sweets and entertainment). There was also enough money to buy my lunch once a week at school should I choose to. On top of this, I had to budget for any birthday or Christmas presents I wanted to buy for my friends or family. Mum would still pay for any school expenses.

It was great having what I thought was lots of money, so on the first week I spent most of my allowance on lollies. But when my stockings got a huge hole in them, I didn't have enough money to replace them. Being a teenager, I told Mum I just couldn't go to school with a huge rip in my stockings! I begged her to loan me some of next week's allowance because I would get in trouble for having holes in my stockings. The school I went to was a posh ladies college, and to not be dressed appropriately was unacceptable. There was a fair amount of peer pressure too – how you looked was very important. I told Mum that because she was choosing not to help me, it would be her fault if I got in trouble with the Head Nun.

'Sylvia,' she replied matter-of-factly, 'it is your responsibility if you are broke – not mine. We agreed that you would be responsible for what you needed to buy. If I rescue you this time, then you will want me to rescue you every time you overspend. You need to learn to put aside money for unexpected expenses.'

If my mother had given me the money to buy stockings, what would I have learned? I could have learned that it didn't matter if I spent my money without considering the future because Mum would rescue me. I could also have learned, at a subconscious level, that when you run out of money it's okay to borrow.

At the time, I didn't appreciate the lesson my mother taught me, but I really learnt from it!

3. LEND MONEY CAREFULLY

Once again, think about the patterns you are establishing with your children from an early age. Rescuing them by lending them money – even for small amounts – could be teaching your child to overspend when they are older.

For example, imagine you give your eight year old child an advance on their pocket money so that they can buy something this week instead of waiting a couple of extra weeks. This is, in fact, a loan.

This seemingly kind act could encourage your child to use credit irresponsibly. When they are young, it is important that they learn to spend less than they earn. Without this lesson, they could be more susceptible to being enticed by 'buy now, pay later' advertising and the unwise use of credit cards. By the time they reach adulthood, this kind of thinking (borrowing instead of saving up) could already be ingrained and difficult to change.

Should you lend money to your kids?

It all depends! I'm not totally against lending your kids money. However, think about your strategy carefully. Write down some rules and stick to them. Don't just think about the here and now – think about how the decision you make now will affect you in the future. For example, will lending money to your children send you broke? If you loan one child money, are you going to be able to do the same for your other children in the future?

Firstly, establish if the money is going to be a loan, a gift or an inheritance advance

Being clear about whether something is a gift or a loan, or an inheritance advance can save much disagreement further down the track.

Don't get the three confused, because the rules are very different. Put simply, loans have to be paid back to the lender, but gifts and inheritances don't.

If it is a gift – give it with no strings attached.
If it is a loan or an inheritance advance – draw up an agreement

Gifts

As stated above, when you give a gift (of money or things) it is important that you give it with 'no strings attached'. Expect nothing in return. You might be disappointed if your child sells a family heirloom, for example, (and you are free to mention this) but in general terms, if you give something to someone, it is theirs to do with it what they want. Even if you disapprove of what your child has done with the money or gift, I think it is important not to voice this opinion.

Generosity and gift-giving are wonderful things that can make a big difference in a person's life. Remember, this isn't about being stingy. But be wise. Be careful that by giving your child gifts, you aren't turning him or her into someone who has a mindset of *entitlement* rather than *thankfulness*.

Loans

When considering lending money to your kids ask yourself:

1. Why have they got into the financial position that they want to borrow money from me?
2. Is it for a 'need' or a 'want'?
3. What could I be teaching them if I say yes or no?
4. Can they afford the repayments?

The rules!

- Don't lend them money for luxury items – i.e. things they don't actually need.
- Do a spending and savings plan with them (a budget) to see if they can afford to repay a loan.
- Don't lend them money if they aren't prepared to agree to the conditions.
- Be clear it is a loan and that you expect it to be paid back. You need to draw up a simple contract, and have both parties sign and date it before the money is given. Many family feuds can be avoided if a contract is drawn up before a loan is given.

I learned the valuable lesson of having a written agreement from my dad, who lent me money for a deposit on a house. I only needed the loan for about a month, because I was selling a car which would give me enough money to repay him immediately. I remember disagreeing with him about the need for an agreement, but he insisted that until I was prepared to agree to the terms of the loan in writing, he wasn't giving me the money.

As I am number six of seven children, I had seen him enacting this policy with my brothers and sisters in the same way... no signed agreement... no money! He also jokingly told me to read the agreement carefully before signing it – just in case he had made a typing mistake and got the payment amounts wrong. Otherwise, I could be signing myself up to payments I couldn't possibly make!

Inheritance advances

Some people choose to give their children an inheritance advance for significant purchases, such as a deposit on a house. In this situation, I think it is a good idea to make all family members aware of the terms of the agreement so that there aren't any surprises when the will is read. It is also necessary to give clear instructions to the executor of the will so that he or she is aware that one person will inherit less due to the advance that has already been received. I recommend that you get professional legal advice if you are planning to head down this track.

When my dad was visiting us from Australia, our car broke down! The problem was that we lived three kilometres from public transport and were a single income

> family with preschool children. Finding funds to purchase a new vehicle or get the old one fixed was a challenge. My father decided to give me a small advance from my inheritance so that we could buy a new car. Dad sent a letter to each of my five brothers and my sister to let them know what he had done. When he passed away some years later, the will made it clear my inheritance had been reduced by that amount. In the end, my brothers and sister were very generous and said that they were happy for me to receive my full inheritance, turning the advance my father had given me into a gift.

The agreement

I'm not a qualified lawyer, so I'm not au fait with all the ins and outs of drawing up agreements. But I can suggest a few basic things to include. If the loan involves a large amount of money, though, I strongly suggest you consult with a qualified lawyer.

Here are the basic things to include in the agreement:

- The date of the agreement
- Who is lending the money
- Who is borrowing the money
- How much the loan is for
- How much the repayments will be
- How often the repayments will be
- When the loan will be settled
- Consequences for non-payment

It is also important to have a way of recording when money is repaid so that everyone is clear on the situation. Draw up a page with the following columns left to right.

- Date paid
- How much paid
- Balance of loan
- Initials of lender
- Initials of borrower

Use a spreadsheet to work out how long it is going to take to repay the loan.

When loaning money, make the conditions reasonably strict so it is clear that repayment is a serious priority and not a walk in the park.

You may think that this is over the top. But I can speak from personal experience as a budget advisor. If families or friends who borrowed or lent money followed this procedure, many family fights and soured relationships would be avoided.

When I was doing my counselling training, I worked in a voluntary role at a hospice to gain counselling hours towards my diploma. My supervisor used to say the best and worst in families always comes out at weddings and funerals!

One case I remember in particular was of a client who came for grief counselling. This young man was devastated when he found out his father's estate had not been divided equally between the four children. The other three children had been given a much larger percentage, and the estate was quite sizable after the family home had been sold.

The father had attached a memorandum to the will explaining the reason why he had not treated his children equally. The memorandum stated that in his lifetime, the father had made many loans to his son, none of which had been repaid. So because of this, the father had decided to reduce his son's inheritance. The heartbreaking thing was that the loans that had been made were relatively small compared to the percentage the son had lost from his father's estate.

On counselling this young man, it appeared there had been a level of misunderstanding while the father was alive. The son had assumed that a number of the loans given to him had been gifts.

More on lending your kids money

When our son wanted to borrow money from us a few years ago for car repairs, we looked at why he needed money, what it was for and what lesson he might learn (either positive or negative) if we gave him a loan.

I had noticed that some of his friends had borrowed money from their parents and were paying it back in small amounts, such as $20 per week, when they were living at home, working and not paying board. I noticed they were spending their money on alcohol and fast food, and that paying back debt was not their top priority.

We decided to lend our son the money with some conditions. When he got a job (he was between jobs after studying), he would have to pay the loan back in regular amounts that consisted of 50 percent of his wages, and would still have to pay board as well. Paying us back would be a priority. We drew up a contract that included these conditions, and my husband, our son and I all signed it. We also explained to him how much the interest would have been had he got a commercial loan, but we didn't charge him interest.

As soon as he got a job, he paid us more than the agreed minimum weekly amount so that he was able to clear the debt as quickly as possible. Once he had completed the repayments, he immediately diverted the same regular amount into his savings, with the aim of buying another more reliable car without getting into any further debt.

From this experience, our son learnt that it is good to help others (as we helped him). He also learnt about contracts, the bondage of debt and was aware of how interest could have increased that burden. He learnt that by saving, he could buy a car without any debt – which saved him future interest costs.

4. DON'T GO GUARANTOR

As I think about writing this, I can almost hear you saying, 'But, I want to help my kids. I don't like saying no.'

As parents, we have a lot of love for our kids and we want what's best for them. Sometimes though, that means making a tough call to ensure that they continue to grow through their life experiences and that you ensure your own financial security.

With that in mind, if you want to remove one way that your kids could send you broke, then don't go guarantor for them.

There's an old Hebrew proverb that warns about the dangers of going guarantor. I like the way it's put in this contemporary translation:

> *'Don't gamble on the pot of gold at the end of the rainbow, hocking your house against a lucky chance. The time will come when you have to pay up; you'll be left with nothing but the shirt on your back.'* (Proverbs 22:26&27, *The Message*)

So in other words, don't guarantee another person's debt or put up security for someone else, because if you do, you could lose your house, your car and the bed from under you. You are putting your financial security (and their future inheritance) at risk, if you act as a guarantor for your child's debt.

Another risk involved in being guarantor is that if your child defaults on the loan (even a smallish loan) and doesn't pay, and you find you can't make the repayment either, then you could lose your own good credit rating.

Even worse, you could sour a treasured relationship. As sad and as difficult as it is to lose your hard earned money, the real tragedy is when you lose a good relationship with your kids.

Avoiding taking on the risk for another person's debt is an excellent principle for all financial dealings, and it's a message you can pass on to your kids as well. Tell them not to go guarantor for anyone or let their name be used to secure credit. If the person can't get credit (or open an account with a telephone or electricity company, for example) in their own name, then there is probably a good reason why.

Some kids really know how to pull at their parents' heart-strings, so be on your guard against manipulation. Some children will say things like, 'If you loved me, you would guarantee my loan so I can get what I want.' You'll need to show some backbone and learn to say no! Tell them your actions will help them in the long run. They may not thank you for it at the time – but they will in years to come.

From early on, our kids knew our feelings about acting as guarantor on their debts. They never asked because they knew the answer would be no! And because the real answer is to avoid dumb debt altogether, we used to tell them they would need to save for what they wanted to buy.

CONCLUSION

Realise that your children will always be your children but they will not always *be* children. Make sure you, and they, know the difference.

An adult takes full financial and emotional responsibility for themselves.

You cannot change the past. If you realise you have been a rescuer and it isn't working, make a change today and help to secure your future.

If your family has been torn apart through disagreements about money, then do what you can to mend these bridges. A little bit of forgiveness goes a long way. Perhaps you are harbouring a grudge towards people who have ripped you off. You might just need to let it go – life is too short and relationships with your family are too important to stay angry all the time. Forgive them and set yourself free.

Perhaps you have realised that you haven't always acted responsibly with money, or been a great role model for your kids; forgive yourself and start doing things differently.

Your job as a parent is to raise financially responsible kids so they don't send you broke! If your kids are already adults and you still feel they are draining your finances – then do something different.

When it's all said and done, it's up to *you* to stop your kids sending you broke.

PS: What to do if it's too late

As we have seen, there are things you can do from an early age to stop your kids from becoming KIPPERS and sending you broke. But what if you've already found yourself in financial difficulties because your kids, whether they are still at home or living in the wide world, are draining your resources? Worse still, what if they've already sent you broke?

The following information can help, and it is also useful information to pass onto your adult kids if they have ended up in financial difficulty.

Get Budgeting Help

If you feel like you are drowning in debt and your kids have nearly sent you broke, start by doing a household budget. *The New Zealand Household Budget Kit*, which I have written, is an effective tool to enable you to create a spending and savings plan for your whole household. But you may need some help from a budgeting service.

Not only can a budget advisor give you the benefit of their specialised knowledge, they can also act as an advocate on your behalf. When I worked as a budget advisor, I found that my clients had often unsuccessfully tried to negotiate more favourable payment terms with their creditors. But when I got on the phone on my clients' behalf, and explained that they had come for help to the budgeting service, the creditor was suddenly more accommodating.

If you need outside help – don't delay.

In New Zealand, and some other parts of the world, Christians Against Poverty (www.capnz.org) are a wonderful organisation who can help if you have unmanageable debt.

In New Zealand, the New Zealand Federation of Family Budgeting Services (www.familybudgeting.org.nz) is another service who can help.

The Salvation Army is also a wonderful organisation that often helps people with budgeting and practical help.

I also recommend www.sorted.org.nz. There is a wealth of information on that website and they have a number of very useful calculators for things like setting a budget, saving and getting out of debt.

When you are determined to get out of debt, a debt elimination programme really works. The first place to start is to decide on a 'debt accelerator' amount. This is added to what you are already paying on a debt, so that you can get rid of the debt more quickly. As soon as you have paid off a debt, add the regular amounts you were paying to the repayments on the next debt. It won't be long before you start to see positive results and gain momentum.

So don't give up! You can get back on your feet.

Dedication

To Jesus,

Because of his work in me, Jesus has been able to do super-abundantly far over and above all that I have asked for or even imagined. (Adapted from Ephesians 3:21, The Bible).

Other books by Sylvia Bowden

How to Stop Your Kids from Going Broke

How often have you read a book or come away from a seminar and thought, 'Ok that's good – but how do you do it?'

This book is the 'how to do it' on teaching your children some essential money skills that will help stop them going 'broke'. It is designed to educate you, your children, and your children's children. It will encourage interaction, provoke frank conversations and give you the odd 'ah ha!' moment of realisation.

New Zealand Household Budget Kit

Everybody wants to find better ways to budget and save, and the *New Zealand Household Budget Kit* provides the solution. It has been designed with modern households in mind and is an extremely useful tool for families, flatmates, couples and any combination of people living together.

Includes easy to follow directions, tear out forms to photocopy and fill in, debt elimination strategies and more…

Visit www.silbo.co.nz for more information

Made in United States
Troutdale, OR
11/03/2026

56844880R00090